Violence against Women and Girls

Understanding Responses and Approaches in the Indian Health Sector

Edited by Sangeeta Rege,
Padma Bhate-Deosthali, and
T K Sundari Ravindran

Routledge
Taylor & Francis Group

LONDON AND NEW YORK

First published 2020
by Routledge
2 Park Square, Milton Park, Abingdon, Oxon OX14 4RN

and by Routledge
52 Vanderbilt Avenue, New York, NY 10017

Routledge is an imprint of the Taylor & Francis Group, an informa business

British Library Cataloguing-in-Publication Data
A catalogue record for this book is available from the British Library

Library of Congress Cataloging-in-Publication Data
A catalog record for this book has been requested

ISBN: 978-0-367-13472-3 (hbk)
ISBN: 978-0-429-28546-2 (ebk)

Typeset in Sabon
by Apex CoVantage, LLC

Contents

Figures

Tables

Boxes

Contributors

K Ajitha: A renowned social worker and human rights activist, Ajitha is a founding member of the Anweshi Women's Counselling Centre and has been its president since its inception in 1993. Her passion for justice and livelihood opportunities for women led her and her colleagues to set up a tailoring shop, which has become an active member of Kerala Sthree Vedi. In January 2005, she was appointed chairperson of the defence committee formed to challenge, in the Supreme Court, the disastrous High Court verdict on the Suryanelli sex racket case involving a 16-year-old girl who was sexually tortured by nearly 42 persons.

Prarthana Appaiah: With a Master's in Business Management, Prarthana moved to the social sector after more than ten years in the corporate sector. She has worked on domestic violence and engaging health systems and self-help groups to respond to survivors of domestic violence. She is a gender trainer and trained counsellor. She consults with St John's Research Institute, Bengaluru. She has been project coordinator for a behavioural economics intervention, assisting couples dealing with violence and alcohol abuse.

Ramesh Awasthi: An alumnus of the Indian Institute of Technology, New Delhi, Ramesh received a Master's in Economics from Meerut University. Ramesh has been active in struggles related to civil liberties in India since the early 1970s. He co-founded Mahila Sarvangeen Utkarsh Mandal (MASUM), a rural women's organisation, in 1987, after living in a drought-prone rural area for five years, and has been its co-convenor since. He spent one year in the Department of International Health at Johns Hopkins University in Baltimore as a visiting fellow. He has made a significant contribution to the development sector through his community-level interventions in women's empowerment, economic empowerment of rural communities, child labour, and minority rights. He has been actively involved in participatory reviews and capacity-building of NGOs at the national level. He is currently on the governing board of the Foundation for Research in Community Health (FRCH) and is chairperson of the ethics committee of the Maharashtra Association of Anthropological Sciences (MAAS).

P Balasubramanian: A social scientist with a PhD in Population Studies, Balasubramanian is Executive Director of the Rural Women's Social Education Centre (RUWSEC), an organisation working on women's health, gender equality, and sexual and reproductive health issues. RUWSEC is based in Thirukazhukundrum, near Chennai. Balasubramanian has been working with RUWSEC as research coordinator since 1998. His experience is in researching and documenting population, gender, and sexual and reproductive rights of young people and women. He is also programme manager of community-based field programmes on sexual and reproductive health. His work mainly involves training grassroots workers, youth leaders, and healthcare providers on violence against women, young people's sexual and reproductive health and rights, and research techniques, tools, and data collection. He has managed several large-scale studies and community-based intervention research projects. He has published more than 25 research articles in peer-reviewed journals at the national and international level.

Padma Bhate-Deosthali: Padma has 20 years of experience in research, training, and policy advocacy in the areas of gender-based violence, gender in medical education, health policy research, regulation of the private health sector, and women and work, with a focus on health and human rights. She is Senior Advisor at the Centre for Enquiry into Health and Allied Themes (CEHAT) and Consultant at Care India Bihar. Padma has a PhD from the Tata Institute of Social Sciences, and her doctoral thesis (2017) was titled "Understanding gendered patterns of burn injuries and response of hospitals in Mumbai." She has several publications in peer-reviewed journals. She led CEHAT as its director for 11 years, during which time the organisation produced a significant body of research and impacted policy and practice. Padma was a member of the GDG-WHO steering group for developing policy and clinical practice guidelines for responding to violence against women. She was a member of the Ministry of Health and Family Welfare National Committee charged with drafting *Guidelines and Protocols: Medico-legal Care for Victims/Survivors of Sexual Violence* in 2014. She coordinated the setting up of Dilaasa, a public hospital-based crisis centre for domestic violence in Mumbai.

Nayreen Daruwalla: Nayreen has a PhD in Social Psychology. She has 22 years of experience working on gender-based violence. She developed the Prevention of Violence against Women and Children programme at the Society for Nutrition, Education & Health Action (SNEHA), a non-profit working on public health issues in Mumbai. She serves as the director of SNEHA, leading the programmes on adolescent health and sexuality and prevention of gender-based violence with communities in urban informal settlements. Her expertise is in conceptualising prevention of violence models for adaption and replication in low- and middle-income countries, focusing on mental health and violence and community mobilisation and intervention. Past projects include partnerships and collaborations with UNFPA, UNICEF, UNDP, Ford Foundation, University College London, and the Wellcome Trust. Currently, Nayreen is designing the scope, content, and measures of effect of a complex intervention for primary and secondary prevention of gender-based violence in India. She co-conceptualised and co-directed an art and health public engagement project, the Dharavi Biennale, in February 2012, which was followed by an art exhibition and festival in February–March 2015.

Kameshwari Devi: Kameshwari pursued a Master's in Social Work in 2003 from Bangalore University and received a PhD in 2014. She has more than 14 years of experience in the field of preventive healthcare. She worked for four years as a psychosocial consultant on the Soukhya project, which aimed at developing comprehensive care for survivors of domestic violence. She is the founder of Cancer Care India, a non-profit organisation providing training and services for women affected by cancer.

Keshav Desiraju: Keshav Desiraju has retired from a career with the Indian Administrative Service and in 2013 was Secretary, Health & Family Welfare to the Government of India. He continues to remain engaged with issues in public health, particularly mental illness and mental health, primary health care and community health, and serves on the board of several non-profit organizations in the sector.

Adsa Fatima: A Programme Associate with Sama – Resource Group for Women and Health, Adsa works in the area of gender-based violence and in strengthening the health system response to GBV. She conducts trainings for healthcare providers and representatives of grassroots organisations in different states of India.

Audrey Fernandes: Audrey is one of the three founding trustees of Tathapi Trust (Women and Health Resource Development), Pune. She has over 30 years of experience in the area of gender and health. Over the last two decades, she has led Tathapi's work with rural, urban, and tribal poor communities, primarily in Maharashtra. The focus has been on building socially conscious individuals and institutions and creating a process of change in perspectives and behaviour related to women and health. Tathapi has worked at the macro level on policy change in violence against women, anaemia in women, and women's reproductive rights and sexuality. Audrey has also developed innovative strategies and curricula on body literacy and sexuality that are acceptable within the Indian cultural context.

Donna Fernandes: Donna holds a Master's in Social Work from the Tata Institute of Social Sciences, Mumbai. A founding member of Vimochana and its secretary and coordinator, Donna is an activist, an organiser, and is a deeply committed campaigner for women's rights, human rights, and a violence-free world. She has initiated a unique study and campaign on dowry deaths and investigations of unnatural deaths of women in Bengaluru. This many-layered campaign led to the Karnataka state government's directives on ensuring justice for women with burns and to far-reaching changes in the functioning of the burn ward at the government-run Victoria Hospital. She also initiated the campaign on better conditions in maternity hospitals. Driven by the drastic decline in sex ratios due to the misuse of new reproductive technologies, she initiated the campaign against sex-selective abortions in Karnataka.

V Jithesh: Jithesh serves as the Assistant Director of Health Services, Kerala; PhD Scholar, Achutha Menon Centre for Health Science Studies, Sree Chitra Tirunal Institute for Medical Sciences and Technology, Thiruvananthapuram; and Deputy Superintendent of District Hospital, Wayanad. He holds a Master's in Public Health and an MBBS degree and has over 19 years of experience. He has co-authored several publications.

Chitra Joshi: Chitra is in charge of the Dilaasa Crisis Centre at Bandra Bhabha Hospital. She leads a team of social workers, physiotherapists, and nurses trained in feminist counselling. Chitra has 20 years of experience in providing direct services to VAW survivors and in training health providers and representatives of CSOs. In the past, she has worked with HIV-positive people and blood banks.

Poonam Kathuria: Poonam is founder and director of the Society for Women's Action and Training Initiatives (SWATI), an organisation working at the state and national levels in India on issues related to violence against women and adolescents, their health, and women's access and right to land and governance. For over 20 years, she has played an influential role in ending gender-based violence and promoting women's empowerment and leadership. Her skills range from project design and management to situation analysis, action research, and capacity development. Poonam was awarded the Dame Nita Barrow Distinguished Visitorship 2014 at the Ontario Institute for Studies in Education, University of Toronto, and taught a special course at the university from June to September that year. She has co-edited and written a chapter in an edited collection titled *Indian Feminisms: Individual and Collective Journeys*, published by Zubaan.

Manpreet Kaur: Dr. Kaur is a public health specialist with experience working in the areas of epidemiology, research, and violence against women. She holds a Bachelor's in Dental Surgery (Baba Farid University of Health Sciences, Punjab) and a Master's in Public Health (Panjab University, Chandigarh). Her core areas of expertise include violence against women, research studies on various critical public health issues, and epidemiological data analysis. She has been actively involved in establishing and operating hospital-based crisis intervention centres at district hospitals in Haryana, with an aim of providing holistic care to women and child survivors of all kinds of violence.

Suneeta Krishnan: Suneeta is a social epidemiologist holding a PhD and has 20 years of experience in conducting research and engaging policymakers on the promotion of health and social equity, with a focus on India. Drawing on the frameworks and tools of social epidemiology, biostatistics, and medical anthropology, she has studied the pathways through which poverty, gender, and other social inequities lead to adverse health outcomes, such as unintended pregnancies, HIV/AIDS, and noncommunicable diseases. She has developed and tested novel interventions to promote health and social equity and engaged decision-makers on the translation of evidence into policies and programmes. She served as Country Director of Research Triangle Institute's Indian subsidiary and has held faculty positions at the University of California, San Francisco and Berkeley; the Indian Institute of Management, Bengaluru; the St John's Research Institute, Bengaluru; and the James P Grant School of Public Health in Dhaka, Bangladesh. Since 2016, she has been at the Gates Foundation's India office, where she leads the measurement, learning, and evaluation team.

Nayanatara Patil: Nayanatara has an MBBS degree and a Master's in Public Health. She has been working with the Bengaluru Municipal Corporation in its public health department for the last 22 years. She was the project coordinator for the Soukhya project, coordinating trainings of health providers, conducting monthly review meetings, and reviewing documentation and support provided to women identified as domestic violence survivors. With her keen interest in issues relating to violence against women, she chose to study women's perceptions of domestic violence in the urban communities of Bengaluru.

Preethi Pinto: Preethi has a Master's in Social Work from Mumbai University. She worked as the associate director of the SNEHA (Society for Nutrition, Education & Health Action) programme on prevention of violence against women and children in Mumbai. She oversaw the programme's primary, secondary, and tertiary interventions to prevent violence against women and girls and handled communications, public relations, documentation, and funding. She began her career with Pax Christi International, where she managed the Asia-Pacific network of member organisations, the youth programme, and gender-mainstreaming within the organisation.

Anagha Pradhan: A consultant at CEHAT, Anagha leads interventions to provide quality services to survivors of VAW. She oversees the 11 NHM Dilaasa centres. She is involved in independent research and consults with several organisations. She has extensive experience with NGOs, working with the public sector on health and gender.

Jayalakshmi Rajeev: Jayalakshmi is Assistant Professor at the Department of Public Health and Community Medicine, Central University of Kerala, Kasargod. She is also a member of the advisory committee of the Centre for Women's Studies, Central University of Kerala. Her areas of interest are women and child health and nutrition, gender inequalities in health, health policy, and geriatric and palliative care. She has worked in association with reputed institutions such as the Indian Institute of Technology, Kharagpur; CEHAT, Mumbai; and Monash University, Malaysia. She has published and presented her work in national and international journals and conferences.

Jasodra Rana: Jasoda is a social activist and counsellor working with survivors of domestic violence. She has been a counsellor at the Society for Women's Action and Training Initiatives (SWATI) since 2009. She has been instrumental in shaping SWATI's work around the rural health sector response to VAW. She is an accomplished trainer and an excellent counsellor. In 2017, in recognition of her lifelong commitment to violence prevention, Jasoda received the Woman Exemplar award from the CII Foundation.

T K Sundari Ravindran: Sundari is currently Principal Visiting Fellow at the United Nations University International Institute for Global Health and Visiting Faculty at the School of Public Health, University of the Witwatersrand, Johannesburg, South Africa. She holds a PhD in Applied Economics and served for 20 years as Professor of Public Health at the Achutha Menon Centre for Health Science Studies, Sree Chitra Tirunal Institute for Medical Sciences and Technology, Thiruvananthapuram. She is a member of the governing board of the National Health Systems Resource Centre, Ministry of Health and Family Welfare, Government of India. Sundari is former co-editor of *Reproductive Health Matters* and is currently a member of its editorial advisory board. She has worked in various capacities with the World Health Organization at its headquarters and regional offices. Sundari is a founding member of CommonHealth (India), a national coalition for reproductive health and safe abortion. She is also a founding member of the Rural Women's Social Education Centre (RUWSEC), a grassroots women's health organisation in Tamil Nadu, and has been involved with the organisation in various capacities since its inception in 1981.

Sangeeta Rege: Sangeeta has a Master's in Social Work. She has 18 years of experience in engaging the public health sector on gender-based violence and, more recently, on integrating gender concerns in medical education. She is presently the coordinator of the Centre for Enquiry into Health and Allied Themes (CEHAT), a non-profit working on health and human rights, and leads the organisation in research and interventions on the health concerns of marginalised people. Sangeeta is trained in social science research, advocacy, training, and counselling and led CEHAT's legal interventions to facilitate gender-sensitive medico-legal care for survivors of sexual violence in 2013. She has led the upscaling of Dilaasa hospital-based crisis centres in different states of India and is committed to generating evidence to strengthen the role of health systems in responding to VAW.

K Satyadevi: With Vimochana for the past 20 years, Satya began a campaign for survivors of burns at Victoria Hospital, Bengaluru, in a bid to provide proper medical care at the burn ward. Her relentless work to create awareness amongst medical professionals at the hospital resulted in systemic changes in the treatment of burn survivors. Her focus is on providing medico-legal care along with psychological support and counselling. Satya has been lobbying for the adoption of a Karnataka State Burns Policy that acknowledges the links between burn injuries and domestic violence.

Nikhat Shaikh: Nikhat is a development professional and qualitative researcher with a Master's in Social Work from the Tata Institute of Social Sciences. Nikhat is a master trainer on issues of gender-based violence, with a focus on building the capacity of healthcare providers and law protectors. She has several years of experience in crisis intervention, counselling, and strengthening public systems to respond to gender-based violence. At the Society for Nutrition, Education & Health Action (SNEHA), she supports the research unit in designing and conducting qualitative research and evaluation for evidence-based practice and policy. Her area of research includes community health workers, adolescent health, and gender-based violence.

P Sreeja: Sreeja is a project coordinator at Anweshi. She holds a Master's in Sociology. Violence against women and children is her area of interest. She has been closely involved in implementation of the Anweshi initiative to engage the health sector on VAW.

Anuradha Sreevathsa: Anuradha has an MBBS degree and a diploma in obstetrics and gynaecology. She has worked as a coordinator of reproductive and sexual health programmes and HIV care for over 12 years. She was a consultant at St John's Research Institute for seven years, training healthcare providers of the Bengaluru Municipal Corporation on early identification of women experiencing violence as well as care, support, documentation, and referral. She is currently a consultant with a research team on safe motherhood and with a programme called Invest for Wellness.

Bhuvaneswari Sunil: Bhuvaneswari is Project Lead at the Centre for Survivorship and Rehabilitation, Indian Cancer Society, Mumbai. She has a background in economics and holds a PhD in Public Health Management from the Tata Institute of Social Sciences, Mumbai. She is a steering committee member at CommonHealth, a national coalition for maternal health and safe abortion. She has served in different health research and academic capacities at renowned academic institutions and civil society organisations in India. She is a general committee member at Rural Women's Social Education Centre (RUWSEC) and is actively involved in its work on the reproductive health needs and rights of women at the grassroots level in Tamil Nadu. She is a strong supporter and advocate for safe abortion rights of women. She has a keen interest in exploring feminist ethics of care perspectives on abortion rights and the sexual and reproductive health rights of marginalised women.

Darilyn Syiem: Darilyn has a Master's in English Literature. She taught Communication in English at Shillong Polytechnic for 28 years. She has worked on women's rights issues through the North East Network for two decades. She was previously chairperson of NEN. She has worked on issues of women's reproductive health and rights, empowerment of women in natural resource management, and violence against women. Darilyn is an experienced gender trainer and has advocated for gender mainstreaming in policies and programmes. Her significant contributions have helped build partnerships between NEN and state agencies on gender issues in agriculture and natural resource management. Her efforts also led to convergence between state departments of Meghalaya on issues of gender-based violence, as a result of which a one-stop crisis centre for women facing violence was set up in a public hospital in Meghalaya. Darilyn is now a philanthropist. She is actively involved in a programme on girls' empowerment in village schools in Meghalaya, in partnership with the Girls Empowerment Movement in the US.

Sonia Trikha Khullar: Sonia holds a Bachelor's in Obstetrics and Gynaecology and a Master's in Public Health. She is currently Director, Health Services, Haryana. She is also Executive Director, State Health Systems Resource Centre, and Director, State Institute of Health and Family Welfare, Haryana. She is in charge of the quality improvement initiative for over 330 public health facilities in Haryana, focusing on improvement of processes related to clinical care, upgrading of infrastructure, capture of outcome indicators, and improvement of outcomes for each health facility. Sonia has played a key role in establishing Sukoon gender health support centres at 11 district hospitals to support survivors of sexual- and gender-based violence. Over 5,000 survivors of violence have received medical treatment, emotional and psychological support, legal and police assistance, and protection services at these Sukoon centres. State Health Systems Resource Centre, Haryana, has restructured itself under her leadership to design and implement a more effective, performance-driven, patient-centric health system, with improved quality of patient care.

Deepa Venkatachalam: Deepa works with Sama – Resource Group for Women and Health in Delhi. She has been engaged for many years with issues of gender, public health, ethics, and rights through research, advocacy, and trainings. She has also published papers, essays, and articles on a range of issues. She has been actively involved with the People's Health Movement and other health and feminist spaces.

N S Vishwanath: Vishwanath received a Bachelor's in Medical Sciences from Assam Medical College, Dibrugarh, and honed his clinical skills at various top institutes across India. He later pursued his Master's in Public Health at the Achutha Menon Centre for Health Science Studies, Thiruvananthapuram. He worked with St John's Research Institute in Bengaluru as Project Director for an ICMR- and, later, USAID-funded project on urban women's health known as the Soukhya project, implemented in partnership with the Municipal Corporation of Bengaluru. The aim was to mitigate the harmful impact of domestic violence on married women. The success of the project was recognised widely, and Vishwanath was selected to be part of the International Visitor Leadership Programme (IVLP), run by the US Department of State, for 2015. He was also awarded honorary citizenship in Dallas, Texas, in recognition of his work.

Foreword

We live in unsettled times. India's population is large and restless, and despite the country's wealth of natural and human resources, the process of development, the eradication of poverty, and the promotion of welfare have been slow. The spread of communications and technology has ensured that our youth are highly aspirational even if they have not always been equipped to achieve those aspirations. And even where incomes have increased across the board, disparities in income have grown even more. We are home to the obscenely rich and to the desperately poor. Unachieved aspirations, the inability to negotiate personal and professional spaces, the hold of customary beliefs, and the lack of any sort of hope: these lead to violence, in society, in our homes and families, in work environments, and in public places. Women bear an uncommonly high share of this violence, so much so that "violence against women" is a recognised public health crisis.

This important book, edited by Sangeeta Rege, Padma Bhate-Deosthali, and T K Sundari Ravindran, looks at a range of interventions that seek to address the health needs of women who have faced violence. I was fortunate to be a part of the process that led to *Guidelines and Protocols: Medico-legal Care for Survivors/Victims of Sexual Violence*, issued in 2014 by the Ministry of Health and Family Welfare, Government of India. This book tells us, in detail, what we have learnt since then and what still remains to be done.

There are three major understandings, all of which this book explains. Firstly, to paraphrase the 1993 UN definition, violence against women is gender-based; it results in physical, sexual, or psychological harm to women; and it includes coercion or arbitrary deprivation of liberty. This means that our public health systems ought to be able to provide care at the primary health level to women and girls who have suffered physical or sexual violence in a caring, non-judgmental, and confidential manner. Women who have suffered psychological damage need access to care at the secondary, district hospital level. It means that women and young girls cannot be forced into marriages even if custom and tradition require early and arranged marriages. It means that violence within the home, or within a relationship, cannot be sanctioned.

Secondly, women find themselves discriminated against on several counts. In a powerful indictment, the editors state,

When dealing with domestic violence, it is imperative that structural violence such as class, caste, communal, state and conflict-related violence is not neglected. Gender intersects all these subsystems of organisation and exploitation. Women face a continuum of violence inside and outside the family, such as violence at the workplace and state-perpetrated violence. The response to VAW must recognise this intersectionality and be sensitive to the specific context of, for example, a Muslim or Dalit woman, as she is likely to face discrimination based on gender as well as religion and caste.

Thirdly, it is both a sign of hope and a sign of despair that none of the interventions studied in this book are driven primarily by the public health system. Even the examples described in Model 1 as "interventions institutionalized by the public health system" have come about because of urging by proactive groups such as CEHAT. The other models describe projects that are community- or NGO-led. Public facilities ought to institutionalise and take ownership of the care, counselling, and welfare of women and girls who have suffered violence, even where there is no intermediary civil society or women's group. We should also understand that even if such facilities exist in paying, private hospitals, they are not likely to be of any use to women in distress who find access to healthcare difficult at the best of times.

There are other issues, some of which this book recognises, which need attention. Domestic violence could also target children, both girls and boys; further, it is not only adult women but also LGBTQI persons and sex workers who live with a constant fear of violence. The mental health of women who have faced violence needs a great deal more attention than it receives at present. We also cannot pretend that the perpetrators of violence, usually adult men, do not need a combination of clinical help, counselling, and care. We also need to recognise the close links between domestic violence, alcoholism, and mental illness.

This book focuses on responses within the health sector to occurrences of violence against women, but it cannot be a responsibility of the health sector alone, whether of health policy makers and doctors and public health workers in public facilities or of community- and NGO-led groups working with women's health. We must have in place whatever it takes to provide help to women following violence, but we cannot be seen to be simply reacting to violence when it has occurred. Sociologists, anthropologists, educationists, teachers, counsellors, lawyers, and leaders of the community need to weigh in on this. Violence against women will not cease only because governments frame a policy. This should be a national priority to us as a society, and as a people.

Keshav Desiraju

Chennai, February 3, 2020

Former Union Health Secretary, MoHFW, GoI

Preface

Violence against women as a subject of concern gained international prominence in the late 1990s, an important reason for which is its recognition as a legitimate human rights issue by the United Nations. For over three decades, women's rights organisations and groups have drawn attention to physical, psychological, and financial violence and its impact. The World Health Organization's multi-country study estimates that at least one in three women suffers violence at the hands of an intimate partner (IPV) once in their lifetime. Similar estimates have been reported in India, where one in three married women has experienced IPV at least once in their lifetime (International Institute for Population Sciences (IIPS) and ICF 2017). It is also known to be a significant cause of negative physical and psychological health consequences. Several Indian laws have laid down the therapeutic and medico-legal roles of health professionals to respond to women and children facing violence. Despite these legal obligations, the health sector in India has thus far not been able to create sensitive and comprehensive responses to survivors of violence against women.

CEHAT – a research centre of the Anusandhan Trust, Mumbai – has been engaged in social science research, action, and advocacy for the last 20 years. CEHAT has been the architect of two evidence-based models of healthcare. The first is Dilaasa, a hospital-based crisis centre for responding to violence against women (VAW) and children, established in 2000, and the second is the comprehensive and gender-sensitive medico-legal care for sexual violence, established in 2008. The Dilaasa model conceptualised counselling as a healthcare need and demonstrated how the health system and healthcare providers at different levels could be equipped to identify and respond to VAW. The comprehensive response to sexual violence built on the Dilaasa efforts and worked to eliminate forensic biases from the medical examination of rape survivors and replaced archaic forensic practices with gender-sensitive care as recommended by WHO. Both these models have been recognised by leading international organisations such as the WHO and have been recommended as sustainable and evidence-based models for LMICs. Indian states, as well as civil society organisations (CSO), took a keen interest in these models, and a process of replication and adaption of these models ensued.

During the last decade, different approaches to addressing VAW as a health issue have been tried and tested by CSOs. These range from the establishment of hospital-based crisis centres, building capacities of health professionals to respond to survivors, advocacy efforts to create a health sector response, including changing victim-blaming attitudes of health professionals against women, and establishing links for smooth referrals from hospitals to CSOs so that survivors receive counselling services. Many of these efforts have not been documented. As a research organisation, CEHAT undertook the endeavour of putting together experiences of organisations working with the health sector to address VAW.

The idea of producing a book germinated when Routledge indicated an interest in publishing such a title and took shape through discussions with organisations working on VAW and the members of the scientific committee of CEHAT. The journey with the organisations contributing to this volume started five years ago with consultations in which ideas were exchanged and case studies were shared.

This book is a synthesis of different approaches to engaging the health sector on VAW and is perhaps the first effort in India to bring together the collective wisdom and learning from practice on this important subject. The 13 case studies covered in the book provide examples of health sector responses to VAW at all levels – primary to tertiary health settings. The case studies offer insights into the journeys of CSOs with the health sector as well as health sector–led initiatives, the many challenges faced, and the efforts made to mitigate those challenges. The book locates these case studies against the backdrop of international and domestic developments in addressing VAW as a health issue, including human rights treaties, which spell out the obligations of healthcare providers and governments to mitigate VAW. This book is a useful resource for policymakers, health practitioners, researchers, and activists for understanding the trajectory of responses to VAW as a health issue in India and for learning from the many promising approaches.

Reference

International Institute for Population Sciences (IIPS) and ICF (2017): *National Family Health Survey (NFHS-4), 2015–16: India*, Mumbai: IIPS.

Acknowledgements

This book is a collective effort of several organisations engaged in developing a health sector response to violence against women. The collective journey started with bringing together different organisations that have engaged with the health sector to respond to violence against women (VAW).

We take this opportunity to thank teams from Vimochana, SNEHA, Anweshi, SWATI, Dilaasa, Bhoomika, Ihlyonti, Goa women's crisis centres, Sukoon, Soukhya, Sama, RUWSEC, MASUM, and Tathapi for their consistent efforts in responding to VAW as well as their contribution to this book.

We are thankful to CEHAT's PDC (Program Development Committee) for their scientific review of the manuscript. Special thanks are due to Ms. Aruna Burte for her rigorous review. The book has been in the making for almost four years and has gained from the rich interactions with individuals such as Dr. Seema Malik, former chief medical superintendent of peripheral hospitals; Dr. Kiran Sharma, Adolescent Health Officer of the World Health Organization, India Country Office; and Ms. Sanjida Arora, Research Officer at CEHAT.

We thank Hutokshi Doctor for her excellent editorial support of the manuscript. The readability of the book improved substantially due to her efforts.

We thank Pramila Naik and Sugandha Bajaj for coordinating with the authors and helping the editors keep the deadlines. We acknowledge Sugandha Bajaj for checking the first draft of the manuscript for references. Last but not least, our heartfelt thanks are due to team members in CEHAT and Dilaasa for their constant support and encouragement.

Section 1

Introduction
Violence against women as
a public health issue

Violence, including violence against women, was placed on the international agenda in 1996 when the World Health Assembly adopted Resolution 49.25, declaring violence, particularly violence against women and girls, a public health priority (World Health Assembly 1996). The resolution called upon the World Health Organization (WHO) to initiate public health activities to (i) document and characterise the burden of violence; (ii) assess the effectiveness of programmes, with particular attention to women, children, and community-based initiatives; and (iii) promote activities to tackle the problem at the international and country level. Recognising its role as the lead agency for coordination of international work in public health, WHO committed itself to providing leadership and guidance to member states in developing public health programmes to respond to violence.

The resolution also expressed concern regarding the increase in all forms of violence, particularly domestic violence that is directed mainly at women, child trafficking, and sexual abuse. It emphasised the importance of treating and caring for victims of violence and strengthening services and support. The resolution called upon member states to present their plans for prevention of violence and the response of health systems to violence. At the subsequent World Health Assembly, the director-general expressed satisfaction with the rapid progress in development of a plan of action for a public health approach to the prevention of violence based on scientific data.

Notable advances in public health approaches to violence against women have been made in high-income countries such as the United Kingdom, the United States of America, Australia, Denmark, New Zealand, Hong Kong, and Canada. Interventions to respond to violence against women and girls (VAW/G) include setting up one-stop crisis centres (OSCCs) and screening for VAW/G in health settings as well as strategies such as home visits and health talks. There is also evidence from high-income countries on the effectiveness and limitations of these different approaches.

A review of health system responses from seven European countries found that committed leadership and organic growth from the bottom up are crucial for any intervention to work well and be sustainable. A clear referral pathway and documented protocols are critical. The review found that regular and ongoing training of health professionals is a cornerstone of successful interventions, while setting up a pool of trainers at the facility level is important for sustainability of the response model (Garcia-Moreno et al. 2015).

In India, it was the women's movement that brought the issue of VAW into the public domain in the 1970s. The movement campaigned for changes in law and rallied for the setting up of counselling centres, shelters, and legal aid for survivors (Kumar 1993). Raped or battered women are often left homeless, penniless, and vulnerable to more violence and discrimination. Even in the midst of a conflict situation, however, women are reluctant to speak about the sexual violence they are being subjected to; therefore, the perpetrators are never tried or are acquitted with impunity (Hameed 2005).

Domestic violence is the most pervasive form of VAW in India. When dealing with domestic violence, it is imperative that structural violence, such as that related to class, caste, commune, state, and conflict, is not neglected. Gender intersects all these subsystems of organisation and exploitation. Women face a continuum of violence inside and outside the family, such as violence at the workplace and state-perpetrated violence. The response to VAW must recognise this intersectionality and be sensitive to the specific context of, for example, a Muslim or Dalit woman, as she is likely to face discrimination based on gender as well as religion and caste.

"The personal is political" is a core feminist principle. It means that whatever happens to individual women (even in their intimate relationships) cannot be fully understood without examining the power relations that exist between people – in this case, between men and women. Structures of class and caste, and discrimination based on ability, sexuality, ethnicity, minority status, political belief, or education, intersect and add to the power imbalance between the genders.

One of the earliest campaigns by the women's movement in India was on women's deaths related to dowry demands from marital families and husbands. The movement demanded that health providers carry out a medical examination of all women dying within seven years of marriage. This recommendation was important because there is invariably an absence of witnesses to dowry-related murders of women. Consistent agitations by the women's movement led to the formulation of a law against dowry demands in the 1980s.

In 1979, the Supreme Court's acquittal of two policemen accused of the custodial rape of Mathura, a young tribal woman, caused a national outcry. There was widespread mobilisation of women's groups and civil society organisations (CSOs), and the ensuing years were marked by agitation, mass campaigns, public education, legal reform, and advocacy to raise awareness about these forms of violence and eliminate them. The outcomes of these agitations included amendments to rape laws, the most significant being shifting the onus of proof to the accused in cases of custodial rape. Several other legal reforms have been introduced since. They include Section 498A of the Indian Penal Code (IPC) in 1983, which penalises the husband or husband's family for cruelty against a woman; the enactment of laws pertaining to investigation of dowry deaths and prevention of sati; the Supreme Court guidelines for sexual harassment at the workplace; and the law criminalising sex-determination tests (Bhate-Deosthali, Maghnani, and Malik 2005). The women's movement confronted the health system for its gender-insensitive response to VAW in general and to rape in particular. In 2005, the Protection of Women from Domestic Violence Act (PWDVA) was passed, which expanded the definition of domestic relationships to all women living in a shared household and allowed women the right to protection from abuse, the right to reside in the house, and economic support from the perpetrator of violence.

Several Indian laws laid down the therapeutic and medico-legal roles of health professionals in relation to VAW/G. In cases of unnatural death of women, health professionals were given the responsibility of recording the dying declaration of women succumbing to violence. The PWDVA also makes specific recommendations for the response of health professionals to women and children facing domestic violence. Most recently, further laws to protect children and women from sexual violence have been enacted, including the Protection of Children from Sexual Offences (POCSO) Act 2012 and the Criminal Law (Amendment) (CLA) Act 2013 on rape, which included other sexual offences, such as stalking, voyeurism, and acid attack (Government of India 2005, 2012, 2013). These laws clearly defined the therapeutic and forensic roles expected of health professionals and also mandated private health facilities to provide immediate healthcare to survivors of VAW.

Concern about violence in any form is completely missing in medical and nursing education in India. The specific health needs of survivors and their rehabilitation do not form part of the medical discourse. It is not as if survivors do not reach doctors. Violence, be it domestic violence, rape, communal/caste violence, or police torture, invariably inflicts physical or psychological trauma, or both. Survivors come for treatment, and in extreme cases, victims are brought for post-mortems. Human rights groups have documented the apathy of doctors in several investigations, past and present. The Medico Friend Circle report (2002) after the Gujarat riots found that sexual violence was not recorded in refugee camps or in post-mortem reports. Direct attacks on hospitals during riots and armed conflict are another issue of concern. The Human Rights Watch (HRW 2016) report on police torture in India highlights the collusion of the medical fraternity with the police, by way of their refusal to record injuries caused by torture or investigate causes of death in police custody. The response of the health sector to sexual violence during armed conflict, state repression, or riots is worse than in "normal" circumstances. The sector's response also has a serious effect on the accessibility and availability of health services. Factors such as migration of health providers from conflict zones and breakdown of health infrastructure because of restricted movement of health providers due to curfew affect service delivery.

Even where infrastructure exists, personnel are unwilling to work because they fear for their lives. Political instability hampers health professionals further, as it compromises their neutrality. Health providers are often under pressure to issue reports that cover up human rights violations, particularly in cases of rape. Whether perpetrated by insurgent groups or security forces, there is always an attempt to hush up rape. The lack of standard operating procedures and protocols in examination of victims compounds the problem.

In this larger context, violence against women in India continues to be on the periphery of the health agenda. The medico-legal role of health professionals is confined to the public health system, but the Government of India has not yet taken steps to ensure a coherent health system response to VAW even within the large public health system, so the engagement of the unregulated and commercialised private health sector in responding to VAW seems unlikely. The dominance of the private health sector for both outpatient (80%) and inpatient care (60%) in India makes a compelling case for private providers also integrating a clinical response to VAW/G.

The initiative to engage the health sector has largely come from CSOs in India. Different approaches have been tried and tested in the last decade. These range from establishing hospital-based crisis centres and building capacities of health professionals to respond to survivors to initiating advocacy efforts to create a health sector response, including changing the victim-blaming attitudes of health professionals, and establishing links for smooth referrals from hospitals to CSOs so that survivors receive counselling services. Very few of these efforts have been well documented, making little evidence available on the advantages and limitations of different approaches and which ones are sustainable and can be adopted or integrated by the health system for creation of a comprehensive response to VAW.

Genesis of the book

The work of the Centre for Enquiry into Health and Allied Themes (CEHAT) on violence has addressed issues of violence against women (domestic violence, sex determination and sex selection, and sexual assault), violence against children (investigation into conditions of juvenile homes), violence by state agencies (investigation of torture, police custody deaths, and atrocities by police), and caste and communal violence. The issue of domestic violence was the starting point for CEHAT's work to legitimise human rights issues within the public health system by conducting research and providing services for victims of violence. CEHAT thought that once the public health system became sensitive to this issue, the adoption and incorporation of other human rights issues into the system would be relatively easy.

When Dilaasa, a hospital-based crisis centre for women, was being conceptualised in 2000, CEHAT had prepared a systematic review of various studies on violence against women in India and had begun the process of establishing a women-centred and community-based action and research project in a slum in Mumbai through the Arogyachya Margavar programme (1998–2003). Dilaasa (which means "reassurance") was set up at the K B Bhabha Hospital in Mumbai between 2000 and 2004 and was formally handed over to the Municipal Corporation of Greater Mumbai (MCGM). In 2008, efforts were made to implement comprehensive healthcare for survivors of sexual violence in three hospitals, in addition to K B Bhabha Hospital, and a formal external evaluation of the Dilaasa model was carried out in 2009. The model has since been replicated in many other states, with CEHAT's support in capacity-building and development of standards of care. Since 2009, CEHAT has led a challenging legal advocacy for uniform gender-sensitive guidelines for responding to sexual violence and establishing the right to healthcare for survivors of sexual violence. In 2015–16, Dilaasa was included in the National Urban Health Mission's Programme Implementation Plan, and 11 new Dilaasa centres were set up in MCGM hospitals.

The idea of this book took root in 2014. Though CSOs have been working with the health sector and engaging with it on VAW/G, information regarding these efforts was not available in the public domain. Very little was known about the approaches that worked and those that posed challenges. This prompted CEHAT to invite CSOs from different parts of India to discuss their approaches, strategies, and lessons learnt. CEHAT believed that a consolidation of these experiences would be a learning resource for departments of health as well as other CSOs that may be interested in engaging with the health sector on VAW. Representatives of 13 organisations from different states were invited to the workshop. Presentations were structured according to the nature of engagement with the health sector. The workshop was divided into the following themes:

1   Strengthening referral procedures with hospitals for comprehensive service delivery to women and girls experiencing violence
2   Collaborations with hospitals to set up crisis centres
3   Advocacy to establish the role of the health sector and community engagement models for VAW

Several diverse ways of engaging the health sector emerged, and it was clear that there can be no single approach. There was unanimous agreement on the usefulness of documenting the efforts of these 13 organisations because very little had been published about the perspectives that prompted these initiatives or the lessons emerging from them.

CEHAT invited these organisations to contribute case studies and, as a research organisation, committed to assisting in the development of these studies. Organisational representatives were asked to develop the first draft themselves, as only implementers can provide a first-hand narrative of their experiences. They were provided a structure and outline to formulate their case studies. They were asked to discuss the genesis of their initiative with the health sector, their reasons for working with the health sector, their expectations of the initiative, the extent to which those expectations have been met, and the aspects that remain unaddressed. This was to be followed by a description of the approaches used, such as networking, collaboration to deliver services, advocacy, and training to seek health provider accountability to VAW. We asked the contributing organisations to situate VAW in the larger context of health service delivery, along with the lessons learnt and challenges of working with the health sector.

While the idea of developing a book with all these case studies was being discussed, WHO released the Global Plan of Action (GPA) 2016, a technical document to develop a health systems approach to VAW/G. India willingly agreed to implement the GPA, draw up national plans, and execute a comprehensive response to VAW in the country. CEHAT used this as an opportunity to initiate a national conference in collaboration with the Ministry of Health and Family Welfare (MoHFW) and WHO (India) in 2016, inviting health departments of different states as well as representatives of the 13 case studies to present their efforts in the health sector. The conference was a milestone, as it provided a national platform to disseminate the lessons learnt from these case studies as well as recommendations for uptake of these approaches in the formal health system.

This book is an effort to document the practices and approaches of engaging the health sector on responding to VAW/G.

The book consists of six sections.

The first section lays the foundations, outlining the many dimensions of violence against women and girls in the context of healthcare. It traces the evolution of VAW/G as a public health concern and provides global and national evidence of the extent and nature of VAW. Finally, this section alludes to the commitments made by the Government of India on global platforms such as the GPA. The section facilitates an understanding of the efforts called for at the primary, secondary, and tertiary levels of the health system to respond to violence against women and girls and places the 13 case studies within the context of the different approaches and responses to VAW/G.

Sections 2 to 5 consist of the 13 case studies on the health sector models. These are divided into efforts made by non-state and state agencies.

- Section 2 includes case studies on Iohlynti (North East Network), Bhoomika, Sukoon, and Dilaasa present institutionalised healthcare responses to VAW by different Indian states. They describe the key factors that led to a systems response.
- Section 3 has case studies – of Vimochana, SNEHA, Soukhya, SWATI, and Anweshi – describe their engagement with hospitals to increase awareness of the links between violence and health, provide quality services to survivors of VAW/G once identified by health providers, and coordinate with other sectors, such as the police and legal aid services.
- Section 4 includes case studies by MASUM and RUWSEC present community-led initiatives for prevention of VAW/G. These initiatives

emerged to fill the gap in access to health services for women belonging to marginalised communities. The case studies describe how community women have been trained to run health clinics for reproductive and sexual health and how these clinics have enabled discussion and advocacy within the community on the impact of violence on health.

- In Section 5 we present case studies by Sama and Tathapi. These case studies highlight the importance of advocacy campaigns that encourage the health sector to view VAW/G as a health concern. They also present efforts to mainstream the health sector's response to VAW in civil society health campaigns such as the Jan Swasthya Abhiyan (JSA) and People's Health Assembly (PHA). Finally, these case studies describe their experience of collaborating with private medical associations to place VAW on their agenda.

Of the 13 case studies, most focus on survivors of domestic violence, which is the most prevalent form of VAW/G in India. While Vimochana, Soukhya, and SWATI focus on the response to domestic violence survivors, MASUM and RUWSEC combine response with strategies to prevent domestic violence. SNEHA and Anweshi provide crisis intervention services to survivors of sexual violence. Within the institutionalised healthcare responses, Dilaasa and Iohlynti remain the only efforts to ensure gender-sensitive care for rape survivors.

Section 6, the concluding section of this book, draws attention to efforts required in other sectors to deal with VAW/G. While the 13 case studies provide critical insights to readers on what is entailed in establishing a healthcare response, they also reveal the huge dependency on non-state players to initiate and sustain this response. The case studies also underline the fact that a long-term, multi-sectoral, and comprehensive response to VAW/G must include the police, justice system, and education system.

Definition and prevalence of violence against women

Defining violence against women

According to the "Declaration on Elimination of Violence Against Women" adopted by the United Nations General Assembly in 1993, violence against women is

> any act of gender-based violence that results in, or is likely to result in, physical, sexual or psychological harm or suffering to women, including threats of such acts, coercion or arbitrary deprivation of liberty, whether occurring in public or private life.
>
> (UN 1993)

Violence against women and girls includes but is not limited to (i) physical violence, such as slapping, kicking, hitting, or the use of weapons; (ii) emotional abuse, such as systematic humiliation, controlling behaviour, degrading treatment, insults, and threats; (iii) sexual violence, which includes any form of non-consensual sexual contact; and (iv) female genital mutilation/cutting (FGM/C), which is an act of violence that impacts sexual organs and as such is included under this category of violence (UN OHCHR 1992).

The definition goes on to include forced marriage (the marriage of an individual against her or his will) and denial of resources, services, and opportunities – also known as economic abuse – such as restricting access to financial, health, educational, or other resources, with the purpose of controlling or subjugating a person, as defined in the UN Convention on the Rights of the Child.

The United Nations' reference to "gender-based" violence highlights the links between violence against women and women's subordinate status because such violence is rooted in gender inequalities. Such violence is also tolerated, and sometimes condoned, by laws, institutions, and community norms that discriminate against women and girls (Heise, Ellsberg, and Gottemoeller 1999). Violence against women cannot be understood in isolation of the gender norms, social structures, and roles that influence women's vulnerability to violence.

The two most commonly studied forms of gender-based violence globally have been intimate partner violence (IPV) and sexual violence.

Intimate partner violence is any behaviour within an intimate relationship that causes physical, psychological, or sexual harm. Such behaviour includes acts of physical aggression, psychological abuse, forced intercourse and other forms of sexual coercion, and controlling behavior, such as isolating the woman from family and friends, restricting access to information and assistance, and monitoring movement. In India, women and girls experience abuse not only from the intimate partner but also from other members of the marital and natal family. Therefore, the Indian legal framework refers to "domestic violence," which is defined as any form of violence occurring within the domestic relationship. It includes spousal abuse as well as abuse by marital family, male partner in a live-in relationship, and parental family members. Domestic violence can also take any form – physical, sexual, economical, or psychological violence.

Sexual violence is any sexual act, attempt to obtain a sexual act, unwanted sexual comments, or advances using coercion by any person, regardless of their relationship to the victim, in any setting, including but not limited to home and work. Sexual violence includes rape, defined as physically forced or coerced penetration of the vulva or anus using a penis or other body part or object, or both. It can include other forms of assault involving the sexual organs, including coerced contact between the mouth and penis, vulva, or anus (Jewkes et al. 2002).

The WHO definition of IPV, which is applied for most prevalence studies, does not fully capture the abuse and control experiences of women, as the perpetrators are not only intimate partners but also other members of the marital family. The operational definition of IPV by WHO needs to be expanded if it is to gather accurate measures and inform domestic violence intervention strategies (Kalokhe et al. 2015).

The case studies presented in this book include work with survivors of domestic violence as well as rape survivors. For the purposes of this book, therefore, we will use the umbrella term "violence against women/girls (VAW/G)" and include under it domestic violence and sexual violence.

Global prevalence of VAW/G

The Convention on the Elimination of All Forms of Discrimination against Women was signed by 189 countries, including India, in 1980. The United Nations declared a response to violence against women and girls imperative in 2006 and identified it as a health priority in the WHO guidelines of 2013 (WHO 2013b). Elimination of violence against women and girls in public and private spaces is a target for Goal 5 of the Sustainable Development Goals (SDGs) (UNDP 2015) as well. Domestic violence and sexual violence are the most pervasive forms of gender-based violence, cutting across caste, class, race, religion, and socioeconomic background. Violence against women is a major issue worldwide, with an estimated 35% of women, or roughly one in three, experiencing physical or sexual intimate partner violence or non-partner sexual violence in their lifetime (WHO 2016). The largest proportion of violence against women is intimate partner violence, which includes physical or sexual violence occurring within an intimate relationship, such as marriage or dating (WHO 2013a). The second major type of VAW is non-partner sexual violence, experienced by at least 7% of women in their lifetime (Abrahams et al. 2014). Non-partner sexual violence includes rape, sexual assault, and any other violence of a sexual nature perpetrated by someone who is not the victim's intimate partner (WHO 2013a). The prevalence of physical and sexual intimate partner violence among all ever-partnered women varies across regions. It is highest in the African, Eastern Mediterranean, and Southeast Asian regions, where approximately 37% of ever-partnered women report having experienced physical or sexual intimate partner violence at some point in their lives.

Prevalence of VAW/G in India

The National Family Health Survey (NFHS) and National Crime Records Bureau (NCRB) provide some insight into the occurrence and nature of violence against women in India. Much of the research contributes evidence of the prevalence of domestic violence. Even within domestic violence, the focus is on marital violence. No estimate of violence faced by girls and women from their natal family is available. With regard to sexual violence by intimate partners, the situation is grim. Much of the global literature as well as NFHS data are focused on intimate partner violence, but in India, women experience violence from intimate partners as well as other members of the marital and natal family.

National-level statistics

NFHS is the only national-level source of data on the prevalence of intimate partner violence that includes related indicators. As seen in Table 1.1 between the two rounds of the NFHS in 2005–06 (NFHS-3) and 2015–16 (NFHS-4), the lifetime prevalence rate of intimate partner violence among women of reproductive age (15–49 years) declined from 34% to 28%. Almost one-third of ever-married women (31%) had experienced spousal physical, sexual, or emotional violence by their current husband (for currently married women) or most recent husband (for formerly married women), according to NFHS-4

Table 1.1 Comparison between NFHS-4 and NFHS-3 in relation to intimate partner violence faced by women

Violence faced by ever-married women of reproductive age (15–49 years)	NFHS-4 (2015–16)		NFHS-3 (2005–06)	
	Lifetime prevalence	*Previous 12 months*	*Lifetime prevalence*	*Previous 12 months*
Prevalence of physical or sexual violence	31%	24%	37%	24%
Of above, reported some injury as a consequence of intimate partner violence	25%	25%	38%	42%
Cuts, bruises, or aches	21%	22%	36%	40%
Eye injuries, sprains, dislocations, or burns	8%	9%	9%	10%
Deep wounds, broken bones, broken teeth	5%	6%	7%	8%
Severe burns	3%	4%	2%	2.1%
Sought some form of help	14%	14%	24%	24%
Of above, sought help from police	3%	3%	2%	2%
Of above, sought help from doctor	1%	1%	0.04%	0.04%

Source: International Institute for Population Sciences (IIPS) and Macro International (2007) and International Institute for Population Sciences (IIPS) and ICF (2017), *National Family Health Survey 3 & 4*, Ministry of Health and Family Welfare and International Institute for Population Sciences, Mumbai.

data, and 24% had experienced at least one of these forms of violence in the 12 months preceding the survey.

With regard to sexual violence, NFHS-4 found that 6% of women report having experienced sexual violence at some point in their lifetime, down from 9% in NFHS-3. Among ever-married women aged 15–49 years who have experienced sexual violence, 83% report their current husband and 9% report a former husband as perpetrators. Among the never-married women who reported sexual violence, the most common perpetrators were "other" relatives (27%), followed by a current or former boyfriend (18%), their own friend or acquaintance (17%), and a family friend (11%). Significant percentages of never-married women report strangers (9%) and teachers (3%) as perpetrators.

In 2015–16, NFHS-4 for the first time included attitudes towards intimate partner violence. More than half (52%) of women and 42% of men surveyed believed that a husband is justified in beating his wife for reasons such as showing disrespect for in-laws, being suspicious of being unfaithful, arguing with the husband, neglecting the house or children, going out without telling the husband, not cooking properly, or refusing to have sexual intercourse.

Estimating the numbers

The estimated number of women likely to be experiencing violence (Table 1.2) is calculated here on the basis of reported prevalence of domestic violence in NFHS-4 and the latest figures for total population of women in the 15–49 age group from the United Nations Department of Economics and Social Affairs, Population Division, 2018. Calculated thus, at least 94 million women in the reproductive age group have experienced some form of physical or sexual violence from their partner in their lifetime, and 73 million women have experienced some form of physical or sexual violence in the 12 months prior to the NFHS-4 survey. Eighteen million women are estimated to have reported some injury caused by domestic violence, which brings the critical role of health professionals and health systems to the fore.

As explained in Table 1.1, of all women in India who have ever experienced any type of physical or sexual violence, 86% had never sought help for the violence they experienced. The percentage of women survivors of violence who *had* sought help has actually declined from 24% in 2005–06 to 14% in 2015–16. This is cause for concern, as it suggests a growing "culture of silence" around VAW and underscores the need to create awareness about available services. Among women who have experienced physical or sexual violence and sought help, the most common source of help was the woman's own family (65%). The second most common source of help was the husband's family (28%). Sixteen percent of women sought help from a friend. Among institutional sources of help, the most common is the police (3%), followed by a religious leader (2%). Only 3% have ever sought help from a doctor or other medical personnel (1%), a lawyer (1%), or a social service organisation (1%).

Table 1.2 Estimates of women experiencing violence based on NFHS-4

Violence faced by women of reproductive age (15–49 years) in 2018	Lifetime prevalence NFHS-4	Estimates for previous 12 months NFHS-4
Prevalence of physical or sexual violence	31% (94 million)	24% (73 million)
Of above, reported some injury as a consequence of domestic violence	25% (24 million)	25% (18 million)
Cuts, bruises, or aches	21% (20 million)	22% (16 million)
Eye injuries, sprains, dislocations, or burns	8% (8 million)	9% (7 million)
Deep wounds, broken bones, broken teeth	5% (5 million)	6% (4.3 million)
Severe burns	3% (3 million)	4% (3 million)
Sought some form of help	14% (13 million)	14% (10 million)
Of above, sought help from police	3% (0.39 million)	3% (0.30 million)
Of above, sought help from doctor	1% (0.13 million)	1% (0.10 million)

Source: International Institute for Population Sciences (IIPS) and ICF (2017), *National Family Health Survey 3*, Ministry of Health and Family Welfare and International Institute for Population Sciences, Mumbai.

Note: Using the rates for lifetime prevalence (violence experienced during lifetime) and estimates for the previous 12 months (violence experienced in the last 12 months), the number of women has been extrapolated using total population of women in the 15–49 age group from the United Nations Department of Economics and Social Affairs, Population Division, 2018. Prevalence rates are taken from International Institute for Population Sciences (IIPS) and ICF (2017). Figures in brackets are the estimated number of women for each category.

The National Crime Records Bureau (NCRB), under the Ministry of Home Affairs, Government of India, collects and analyses all data on crime as defined by the IPC. Its annual reports provide information on all crimes registered with the police, including crimes against women. NCRB recorded 129,322 sexual offences against women in 2016, including rape, outraging the modesty of a woman, and attempt to rape (NCRB 2016). NCRB data also showed that a whopping 93% of offenders were known to the victims/ survivors. An analysis of 728 service records of rape survivors coming to hospital found that 79% of survivors were abused by a known person (57% were known persons such as neighbours, teachers, shopkeepers, and so on; 13% were family members; and 6% were abused by the intimate partner) (CEHAT-MCGM 2018). Additionally, NCRB (2016) recorded 7,621 dowry deaths and 110,378 cases of cruelty by husbands. The data on crimes against

Table 1.3 Crimes against women, NCRB data

NCRB data	2014	2015	2016
Domestic violence			
Cruelty by husband	118,866	113,403	110,378
Dowry deaths	8,455	7,634	7,621
Total	127,321	121,037	117,999
Sexual violence			
Rape	36,735	34,651	38,947
Outraging modesty	82,235	82,422	84,746
Attempt to rape	4,234	4,437	5,629
Total	123,204	121,510	129,322

Source: National Crime Records Bureau (2014, 2015, 2016), Ministry of Home Affairs, Government of India.

women from these records are of those women and families who have mustered the courage to register a police complaint. These numbers are therefore representative of women who have entered the criminal justice system, whereas it is widely known that women are more likely to report violence and seek services from counselling centres run by the government or nongovernmental organisations.

Challenges with national data sets

A comparison of NFHS (prevalence) and NCRB (reported incidents) data shows the reluctance of women to seek formal redressal for violence. According to NFHS-4, at least 73 million women had experienced some form of physical or sexual violence in the 12 months preceding the survey. Of these, 18 million women reported some form of injury due to domestic violence, but only 10 million sought help of some sort. Most women first sought assistance from the family. Only 0.3 million sought help from the police. The number of cases of domestic violence registered at NCRB, however, is 0.11 million, which is less than half the number of cases recorded in Table 1.3.

It is pertinent to note, however, that national-level surveys do not record the frequency and impact of domestic violence and sexual violence, nor do they capture the consequences of violence against women leading to suicide attempts or repeat incidents of victimisation. Williamson (2013) points out that building such measures of impact while collecting data enables a deeper understanding of the prevalence of domestic and sexual violence. Population-based national surveys collected by governments of different countries do not consider the number of women and children seeking support from independent domestic violence advocates, health professionals, shelter homes, and social workers, and hence national surveys on prevalence of violence against women and children may not be the most reliable source. Under-reporting of violence against women is also a challenge in large-scale surveys because these are primarily designed for other purposes. These challenges have to be addressed by emphasising the privacy and safety of women and allowing them multiple opportunities to disclose their experiences (Bott, Morrison, and Ellsberg 2005). Special surveys, in addition to large national surveys, are required for this.

Extent and nature of domestic violence revealed by community-based studies

This section presents different studies carried out in communities and health facilities specifically aimed at estimating prevalence of VAW.

Estimates related to domestic violence from community-based studies vary from 18% to 70% (Rao 1997; Mahajan 1990; Jejeebhoy 1998; Visaria 2000; Khot, Menon, and Dilip 2004). These variations can be attributed to differences in definition, methodology, manner in which questions are asked, extent of rapport established, and ways in which data are analysed. Studies conducted by institutions that report high prevalence may be due to a better trained research team that is able to create the necessary environment for the reporting of violence.

A study of pregnant women attending antenatal clinics suggests self-reported physical, psychological, and sexual violence in the previous year at 14%, 15%, and 9% respectively (Varma et al. 2007). Recent evidence from Mumbai public hospitals puts the prevalence of domestic violence during pregnancy at 16.1%, which is comparable to the prevalence of common obstetric complications routinely screened at antenatal clinics (Arora, Bhate-Deosthali, and Rege 2018). A survey of 397 women in rural south India reported that 34% of them had been beaten and forced by their husbands to have sex (Krishnan 2005). A similar survey found that 41% of currently married and 28% of never-married women reported sexual violence in the 12 months preceding the survey. Thirty-three percent of currently married and 40% of never-married women reported seeking help for sexual violence. In the same survey, married women's responses to a hypothetical question about what would happen if they did refuse sex was revealing: 36.7% of married women reported they would be forced to have sex.

A cross-sectional study conducted by Santhya and Jejeebhoy (2007) on unwanted sex among young married women acknowledged that, methodologically, research studies are likely to underestimate sexual violence within marriage because women may experience unwanted sex without physical violence but are less likely to label such instances coercion by the husband.

A study by the International Centre for Research on Women (Pande et al. 2017) draws attention to the high prevalence of intimate partner violence in India as reported by men and women. At the aggregate level, more than half the women (52%) surveyed reported experiencing some form of violence during their lifetime, and three in every five men (60%) reported perpetrating some form of intimate partner violence against their wife/partner. The higher number of men reporting IPV is clear evidence of the social sanctioning of this violent behaviour. The fact that so many men reported perpetrating physical, emotional, and sexual violence on their partners requires attention.

There is growing evidence of the social attitudes that contribute to the high prevalence of gender-based violence. Gender inequality has been cited as one of the major factors associated with VAW (Visaria 2000). Rigid gender roles and norms contribute to violence against women, as violence is used as a tool to maintain the status quo. Moreover, a culture that, in general, justifies violence as a way to resolve issues and conflicts in society also condones violence against women. There is a widely held view that girls and women have a lower status in society and should comply with, and conform to, the defined gender roles of devoted mothers and wives. Several studies have demonstrated that rates of violence against girls and women are higher in societies characterised by such unequal gender roles, where "manhood" is defined in terms of dominance and "womanhood" is constrained by the fulfilment of certain rigid codes of conduct. When such roles are not fulfilled, partner violence may be seen as a justified form of punishment. Close to half of all girls aged 15–19 worldwide (about 126 million) think a husband or partner is sometimes justified in hitting or beating his wife (or partner) under certain circumstances: if the wife argues with her husband, goes out without telling him, neglects the children, refuses to have sexual relations with him, or burns the food (UNICEF 2014).

Impact of violence against women on health

Violence results in non-fatal or fatal injuries: 21% of homicides in Southeast Asia are committed by an intimate partner, with 60% of all female homicides committed by an intimate partner (the figure for male homicides is 1%) (Stöckl et al. 2013). Intimate partners are reported to commit as many as 38% of all murders of women globally. Forty-two percent of women who have been physically or sexually abused by a partner have experienced injuries because of that violence (WHO 2013a). Women who have experienced partner violence have higher rates of several major health problems and risk behaviours. Compared to women who have not experienced partner violence, they have a 16% greater chance of having a low birth weight baby, are more than twice as likely to have an induced abortion, and are more than twice as likely to experience depression. In some regions, they are 1.5 times more likely to acquire HIV and 1.6 times more likely to have syphilis compared to women who do not suffer partner violence (WHO 2013a).

The health consequences of VAW include sexually transmitted infections, miscarriage, induced abortion, stillbirth, low birth weight, preterm delivery, harmful drug and alcohol use, anxiety and depression, self-harm, suicide, and trans-generational recapitulation of violence (WHO 2013a, 2013b). The physical and psychological trauma and fear lead to mental health problems, limited sexual and reproductive control, somatoform conditions, difficulties in seeking healthcare, and loss of economic productivity (Solotaroff and Pande 2014). The two-way linkages between violence and health are also evident in women's lives since ill health and disclosure of illness increase the element of violence in their lives. Women with tuberculosis, mental illness, or HIV/ AIDS are likely to be thrown out of the house and may therefore be reluctant to disclose their disease to their families or get their illnesses diagnosed. If a woman has a white discharge, she may be accused of sleeping with other men; if she falls sick repeatedly, she may not get medical attention. Thus, women are more vulnerable to illness because of their low status in society and low access to adequate nutritious food, rest, and recreation. This in turn increases the probability of violence in their lives. Being dependent on husbands and the marital family for healthcare effectively silences a woman, and when she does get to the health centre, notions of family "honour" and the consequences of speaking out may keep her silent about the violence she experiences. A vicious cycle of violence and ill health is thus set in motion (Gupte 2013).

Health professionals generally consider domestic violence against women a private matter. They believe their role is limited to treating the disease and the physical manifestations of such violence. Violence is often seen as a social or criminal justice problem only and not as a clinical or public health issue. Such a bio-medical approach does not facilitate the disclosure of domestic violence, nor does it elicit an appropriate and useful response from health professionals (Garcia-Moreno et al. 2015). Besides, health professionals, male and female, often share the sociocultural notions that sanction and justify male dominance over women, and these attitudes reinforce violence against women.

Blaming women for the violence faced by them, considering violence part of married life, and believing that women must have provoked the violence are some of the beliefs reflected amongst health professionals as well (Bhate-Deosthali, Maghnani and Malik 2005). Linked to this is a lack of gender sensitivity and failure to understand inequalities, especially gender inequality in health. In addition, health providers may not be sensitive to other forms of discrimination that intersect with gender, such as discrimination based on class, caste, community, sexual orientation, and disability, and may harbour these biases themselves. The disrespect and abuse of women that have been documented in healthcare settings, especially in reproductive health services, further discourage women from disclosing domestic violence to healthcare providers (Khanday 2017). Women health workers, such as doctors, nurses, and front-line health workers (FLWs), are themselves likely to be survivors of violence in their homes or workplaces (Bhate-Deosthali and Rege 2012).

There is compelling evidence of the high numbers of women and girls affected by violence of all forms and the direct and indirect impact of such violence on their health and well-being. Many of the women experiencing domestic and sexual violence seek medical assistance in hospitals and other health facilities. The health sector can no longer overlook the implications of violence against women.

Framing the health system's response to violence against women

Over the last 20 years, many organisations have tried to improve the health service response to gender-based violence in high-, low-, and middle-income countries. Organisations sometimes take small steps, such as providing a single training session for staff. Unfortunately, evidence suggests that without system-wide reforms and support, single training sessions, or even routine screening policies, rarely produce long-term changes in the quality of care for survivors (Bott, Morrison, and Ellsberg 2005).

Growing evidence, and the experience of primarily industrialised countries, suggests that public health programmes, policies, and approaches *can* make a difference.

Although WHO recognised VAW as a global public health priority in 1993, few countries have developed a comprehensive healthcare policy that is integrated into a multi-sectoral societal response to violence against women. Health systems in high-income countries have been able to integrate the response to VAW, but low- and middle-income countries are still struggling to do so. A high prevalence of domestic violence and weak health systems in these countries adds to the challenge.

The public health model places great importance on the prevention of injury and ill health (primary-level intervention), harm reduction (secondary-level intervention), and treatment and rehabilitation (tertiary-level intervention) (Table 1.4). In addition to primary prevention efforts, one cannot

Table 1.4 Level of health system and expected response to violence against women

Level of health system	Expected response to VAW
Primary	• Create awareness about types of violence, health consequences of violence • Create awareness about existing services • Train staff to provide first-line treatment to women • Set up a referral mechanism
Secondary	• Identify and report violence • Provide clinical and forensic care • Set up crisis centres and crisis intervention services through a dedicated department or designated trained staff
Tertiary	• Identify violence, provide clinical and forensic care • Set up crisis centres • Train personnel to provide crisis intervention, rehabilitation, and long-term care • Include training on VAW in the curriculum for medical colleges

Source: Role of health sector in addressing intimate partner violence in India: a synthesis report, International Center for Research on Women (ICRW).

ignore the fact that a large number of women are already accessing the healthcare system for complaints arising from violence. Public healthcare systems therefore also need to plan and implement programmes that provide the social and psychological support much needed by women in crisis as well as programmes that reduce the harm caused by violence. Public health efforts must focus on harm reduction (secondary-level intervention) and treatment and rehabilitation (tertiary-level intervention).

Primary prevention

Primary prevention strategies refer to efforts that can prevent violence from occurring in the first place. Although prevention is a well-established concept in the field of public health, theories and programming for primary prevention of violence against women and girls are relatively new (Garcia-Moreno et al. 2014).

The health system can raise awareness about the need to address violence against women by reporting and publicising data on the prevalence, health burden, and costs of violence and by countering the acceptability of such violence. However, evidence to guide healthcare organisations in primary prevention activities is scarce. Lori Michau and others have reviewed the existing evidence, and they write that most primary prevention involves actions outside of the health sector (Michau et al. 2015).

Within the Indian healthcare setting, health workers at the community level, such as accredited social health activists (ASHAs), auxiliary nurses and midwives (ANMs), and Integrated Child Development Services (ICDS) anganwadi workers (AWWs), can aid primary prevention.

Primary health workers could be engaged in the following activities:

- Activities to help girls and women in the community understand and recognise the forms and consequences of violence. These activities should increase their knowledge about their rights, promote an understanding of what constitutes a healthy relationship, boost their self-esteem, and instil the belief that they do not deserve to be abused.
- Training male health workers to organise educational and awareness-building activities for adolescent boys and men on gender inequality, positive gender roles, and healthy relationships.
- Printing and posting information, education, and communication (IEC) material at all levels of the public health system that sends out the important message that VAW is a public health issue and that women and girls can report violence to public health facilities.

However, front-line workers are already overworked and burdened with too many targets. They are not even adequately remunerated, as they are voluntary workers with absolutely no support from the system. There is evidence that often they are themselves victims of domestic violence and sexual harassment, including rape.

Secondary prevention

Secondary prevention strategies involve efforts to minimise the harm already done and prevent further injury from occurring. Within the healthcare setting, both healthcare and social service providers can play important roles in helping women report the abuses they are facing and in educating women about available medical and social services.

Identification of women and girls who are, or have been, subjected to violence and referral to specialised services where these exist are prerequisites for appropriate treatment and care. The experience of the various models studied indicates that identifying violence calls for training of healthcare providers in understanding the signs and symptoms associated with violence so that they know how to ask about violence and how to respond to it. Providers also need training to carry out proper and thorough documentation of recent incidents of abuse, resulting injuries, and history of violence and to make referrals to the appropriate agency or department for further care and emotional and social support (Rege and Bhate-Deosthali 2018).

The minimum requirements for asking about partner violence include a protocol/standard operating procedure, training on how to ask questions about VAW, a minimum response or beyond, a private setting, assured confidentiality, and a well-defined system of referral. WHO guidelines recommend that all healthcare providers be trained in women-centred first-line support and the ability to respect a woman's right to decide on her own pathway to safety. This approach is consistent with what is known as psychological first aid, a first response to individuals undergoing traumatic events. A supportive response from a well-trained provider can act as a turning point on the pathway to safety and healing.

Tertiary prevention

Tertiary prevention efforts refer to strategies aimed at addressing previous exposures to physical, emotional, economical, and sexual violence and their consequences. Within the public health framework, such strategies would involve the delivery of services such as counselling, advocacy, referrals to other needed social services (such as shelter, legal aid, educational and job training programmes, and medical services), and assistance in negotiating and accessing these different, and often fragmented, service systems. The long-term impact of experiencing violence may call for mental health services that are gender-sensitive and available at the tertiary level.

Healthcare providers – particularly doctors – are in a unique position to identify victims of violence. Not only are they often the first contact for victims seeking treatment, but they are also highly regarded and seen as neutral entities in whom patients can easily confide. This unique position enables doctors to enquire into the current (or most recent) episode of violence as well as the history of abuse by creating a safe environment and providing privacy. Also, doctors are the only individuals within the public health system with the authority to register medico-legal cases, conduct autopsies, collect important forensic evidence, and carry out post-mortem examinations. All these procedures are necessary to prove the occurrence of violence and punish the perpetrator.

Responses to VAW in India by feminists, community-based organisations, multilateral agencies, and international non-governmental organisations

The earliest wave of Indian feminism was triggered in the 1970s and 1980s by the rapes of women by the police and feudal landowners. These rapes were understood simultaneously as class, caste, and women's issues. The issue of domestic violence came into the public domain at the same time, with attention focused on the large number of dowry deaths, or bride-burnings, and the physical abuse and battering of women. Women also faced domestic violence unrelated to dowry demands. The silence and social stigma around domestic violence began to be broken during this period. The women's movement used the slogan "The personal is political" to demystify the "private" space – that is, the home. This made it possible for individual women to come forward and share their agony and pain. The movement asserted that all women have the right to violence-free lives and that domestic violence inhibits women from realising their rights and full potential in all aspects of their lives – social, economic, and political.

In addition to raising awareness about violence against women, autonomous women's groups, along with NGOs, were the first to establish some kind of infrastructure and services to care for and support women survivors of domestic violence. The state also responded to the growing pressure created by the sustained campaigns during the 1980s and 1990s. This led to the establishment of free legal aid cells, family counselling centres, family courts, and special cells at police stations in the city of Mumbai, creating several spaces that women and girls surviving domestic violence could approach. These efforts helped individual women and, to an extent, sensitised public systems to respond to the issue of domestic violence.

The relationship between the women's movement and the health system has been a complex one. In fact, it has been quite antagonistic at points – in its confrontation of coercive population policies, for instance. The women's movement confronted the system's insensitivity to the reproductive and sexual health needs of women and its failure to understand broader gender issues. The women's movement and the health movement in India highlighted several lacunae in the existing health system, such as how the failure to document important forensic evidence in the event of sexual assault could severely limit the survivor's ability to get justice.

While the serious health consequences of domestic violence for women are well researched and well established, the role of the public health system in responding to the issue has not received adequate attention. Therefore, although violence by the health system was a serious issue within the women's movement, little effort was made to work closely with the system until Dilaasa – the joint initiative by CEHAT and MCGM – was set up in 2000. The public health system is an important site for the implementation of anti-domestic violence intervention programmes, as it is often the first contact point for victims and survivors who approach healthcare providers for treatment of physical and psychological post-violence trauma. Dilaasa crisis centres train hospital staff to respond to VAW/G and equip them to deal with survivors as part of their roles and responsibilities. The model includes crisis intervention services and psychosocial support, which is currently missing in the health sector.

The response of health professionals to cases of sexual violence is another key concern. More often than not, their role is restricted to forensic examination and collection of evidence. They are unaware of the therapeutic role they need to play, especially with regard to aspects such as psychological first aid and treatment. Even when carrying out forensic functions, health professionals restrict examination to an assessment of the genitals. A tendency to over-emphasise genital and physical injuries has been noted amongst health professionals (Bhate-Deosthali, Maghnani, and Malik 2005). Unscientific practices of examination, in the form of the finger test to determine hymenal status and recording the height and weight of the survivor to examine the possibility of resistance, are the norm in medico-legal examinations of sexual violence (Bhate-Deosthali 2013). CEHAT's intervention model, offering a comprehensive response to sexual violence at three hospitals in the Mumbai Municipal Corporation region, was designed to address these gaps and train health providers to implement the medico-legal protocol designed by WHO (WHO 2013b). These protocols have enabled a comprehensive response and have helped overhaul the entire procedure. The protocols include prioritising therapeutic care, implementing informed consent, carrying out a gender-sensitive medical examination, and providing reasoned medical opinion. It was important to replicate the model implemented in the three municipal hospitals across the state of Maharashtra. Equipped with evidence of the effectiveness of this model, CEHAT, in collaboration with Lawyers Collective, intervened in a legal case related to establishing uniform protocols for medico-legal care of rape survivors in Maharashtra. It also presented evidence emerging on the use of these protocols for the Justice Verma Committee report (JVC Report 2013). Recognising the need for urgent reforms in medico-legal care for rape survivors, MoHFW (2014) developed comprehensive protocols for a healthcare response to rape survivors. This was a landmark move, as it was the first time the health ministry acknowledged VAW/G as a health issue and took responsibility for the creation of protocols that were issued subsequently to all Indian states.

Legal mandate for health professionals in responding to violence against women

The historic campaign by the women's movement, along with the mothers of women who died in what were described as "stove bursts" and recorded as "accidents" by the police, demanded an investigation of these deaths as murder. In the mid-1980s, this went on to become a nationwide campaign led by feminist groups. Several legal amendments were pushed through during this period, and laws related to dowry deaths and abetment to suicide were formulated (Jaising 2014). As a response to the daily headline of women dying of "stove bursts," in 1983 Section 498A was introduced in the IPC whereby cruelty by a husband and his family against a wife was made an offence. The legal provisions under the IPC – Section 304B (dowry death), Section 498A (cruelty), and Section 306 (abetment to suicide) – mandate a responsibility of doctors to inform the police of all cases of burn injuries, carry out the necessary medico-legal documentation, and, in case of death, conduct a post-mortem examination (Agnes 2005). The medico-legal role of the doctor in cases of reported burn injuries or deaths caused by burns was thus well entrenched in the criminal justice system.

In all other cases of assault causing injury, whether simple or grievous, the medical profession was responsible for documenting evidence, either oral or documentary. Oral evidence refers to when a doctor attends court when summoned. Documentary evidence includes a medical certificate or medico-legal reports like injury certificate, post-mortem report, age estimation, and dying declaration. A doctor's medical evidence includes preliminary data on name, age, and address; the findings on examination; and the opinion or inference drawn by the doctor.

The Protection of Women from Domestic Violence Act (PWDVA) 2005 is landmark legislation that recognises domestic violence as a punishable offence, extending its provisions to women in live-in relationships. It provides civil remedies such as the right to residence, protection from abusers, and compensation orders, as well as a woman's right to the matrimonial home, in addition to legal recourse. Defining domestic violence as "any act that harms, injures, endangers, the health, safety, life, limb or well-being of the person or tends to do so," the PWDVA includes "physical, sexual, verbal, emotional abuse or intention to coerce her or any person related to her to meet any unlawful demand for dowry or any other property/valuable security."

The PWDVA was the result of cumulative efforts made by the women's movement to provide specific remedies for women experiencing domestic violence, whereby they could approach the state directly and get a protection order to stop violence in the home without having to put the husband behind bars or having to leave the matrimonial home to escape violence (Jaising 2014). The act recognises public health facilities as service providers and mandates that all women reporting domestic violence receive free treatment and information on or appropriate referral to protection officers. The rules for implementation of the PWDVA mandate appointment of special officers, called protection officers, who can receive complaints of domestic violence and facilitate specific protection or restraining orders from the magistrate's court to stop violence. Besides this cadre, the law seeks registration of service providers who can offer counselling, shelter, and legal aid services to survivors and support them through grants. Public and private medical facilities have been termed "service providers" under this law, and they are expected to be trained to record complaints related to domestic violence and make appropriate referrals to protection officers or other services depending on women's needs.

In case of sexual violence, too, there is a clear role defined under criminal law that mandates the role of medical professionals in medical evidence collection and documentation. The Protection of Children from Sexual Offences (POCSO) Act 2012 and Criminal Law Amendment 2013 have defined sexual violence as inclusive of all forms of sexual acts, thus expanding the definition of rape. Until then, only peno-vaginal penetration was considered rape. These legal provisions have made it mandatory for all medical facilities (public and private) to provide treatment and psychological support. Taking cognisance of the new legal provisions, and the critique of the insensitive and archaic forensic practices in dealing with cases of sexual violence, the MoHFW's National Guidelines and Protocols, issued in 2014, recommended gender-sensitive examination, relevant evidence collection based on history, and banning of the two-finger test and irrelevant comments on hymen and size of vaginal introitus. Another significant direction from the ministry is for provision of medical care, including first-line psychological support, as recommended by WHO in 2013 through its clinical and policy guidelines for responding to IPV and sexual assault.

Locating VAW in policy and programmes in India

Despite the legislation on violence against women and girls and the explicit role of the health sector spelt out therein, several challenges remain in the implementation of these roles on the ground. One reason for this is the lack of technical and financial resources for implementation of health sector roles. MoHFW recognised VAW as an issue only after the massive campaign that followed the brutal sexual assault and murder of a young physiotherapist in December 2012 (the Nirbhaya case). Though the health ministry formulated comprehensive medico-legal guidelines for survivors of sexual violence in 2014, and issued them to all states, several states have not implemented these protocols five years on. The other concern is that these protocols cover only sexual violence. No protocols for care of those experiencing domestic violence have been developed or issued by MoHFW, despite its pervasiveness.

In fact, WHO's clinical and policy guidelines of 2013 were issued to prompt a coherent health sector response in low- and middle-income countries. The

WHO guidelines (WHO 2013b) recommend that ministries of health adopt a variety of models for provision of care at different levels of the health system, rather than being bogged down with a single model for the entire country. The guidelines also recommend the integration of VAW within clinical care at all levels, from primary to tertiary, notwithstanding the presence of a full-fledged OSCC. This is an important recommendation, as low- and middle-income countries have limited resources across various sectors and OSCCs are resource-intensive.

India is committed to the Global Plan of Action (GPA), adopted at the 69th World Health Assembly in May 2016, to strengthen the role of the health system within a national multi-sectoral response to intimate partner violence, in particular against women, girls, and children. The GPA will contribute to the achievement of the SDGs, including Goal 5 (Achieve Gender Equality and Empower All Women and Girls), Goal 16 (Promote Peace, Justice and Inclusive Societies), and Goal 3 (Ensure Healthy Lives and Promote Well-being for All at All Ages).

The Global Plan recommends action in four strategic directions:

1 Strengthening health system leadership and governance
2 Strengthening health service delivery and health workers'/providers' capacity to respond to violence, in particular against women and children
3 Strengthening programming to prevent interpersonal violence, in particular against women and girls and against children
4 Improving information and evidence

The WHO has also laid down clear indicators for monitoring progress made by countries under the GPA:

- Inclusion of healthcare services to address IPV and comprehensive post-rape care in national health or sexual and reproductive health plans or policies, in line with WHO guidelines
- Development or updating of national guidelines or protocols for the health system response to women experiencing violence, consistent with international human rights standards and WHO guidelines
- Provision of comprehensive post-rape care in a medical facility in every territorial or administrative unit, consistent with WHO guidelines
- Having a national multi-sectoral plan that includes the health system and that proposes at least one strategy to prevent violence against women and girls
- Carrying out a population-based, nationally representative study/survey on VAW or including a module on violence against women in other population-based demographic or health surveys within the past five years, disaggregated by age, ethnicity, socioeconomic status, other

Notwithstanding these global commitments since 2013, VAW/G found place in India's National Health Policy (NHP) only in 2017. The NHP (MoHFW 2017) mandates that health establishments must offer immediate care to survivors of VAW/G and that the health sector must carry out gender-sensitisation activities with health providers to equip them adequately. Several promising interventions in the health sector exist. While some demonstrate how health providers can be equipped to respond to women and girls, others demonstrate ways of integrating a response to VAW/G in the system.

One of the earliest systems interventions is the Dilaasa crisis centre, set up in 2000 in a Mumbai municipal hospital and now replicated in several states across India. An external evaluation (Bhate-Deosthali, Ravindran, and Vindhya 2012) of Dilaasa found it an evidence-based and sustainable hospital-based model for responding to domestic violence and sexual violence. It was envisioned as a department of the hospital, integrating psychosocial services related to VAW/G within other hospital services. Key functions of the department include collation of aggregate monthly data on the number of women and children receiving services, nature of health consequences related to VAW/G, and nature of services accessed by survivors. A monitoring committee comprising the hospital administration as well as Dilaasa department head oversees Dilaasa's activities.

Dilaasa ensures police support (making telephone calls to police stations when survivors want to register a complaint), social support (linking survivors to shelters, children's institutions, hostels, and financial aid institutions, amongst others), and legal support (putting survivors in touch with lawyers and supporting them during court trials). Dilaasa also has strong linkages with child welfare committees (CWCs).

Dilaasa's case records reveal that 60% of the women who come to the centre have not reported domestic violence to any formal agency – police or NGO. As health professionals are trained to understand the signs and symptoms associated with violence, identify abuse, and refer cases to Dilaasa, women are reached at an earlier stage of abuse, preventing further harm. One-third of the women who sought the services of the crisis centre had been victims of violence for fewer than two years. More than 50% were able to seek services within six years. A public hospital-based crisis centre also serves a larger number of women – usually twice the number served at other counselling centres. Dilaasa registers about 250 new users every year; 50% of the new users follow up for counselling services as well. Some of these women have reported that the location of the services in a public hospital makes access to domestic violence intervention programmes easier, as they can come to the hospital on the pretext of their own or someone else's health problem (Bhate-Deosthali, Ravindran, and Vindhya 2012).

Besides Dilaasa, different models to engage the health system exist. Table 1.5 provides a glimpse of the models set up in tertiary- and secondary-level hospitals. The pathway for women to these centres is unique, as they

Table 1.5 Models at various levels of the health system in states

Name	Location	Staffing	Services	Referrals	Funding	Components
TERTIARY LEVEL						
Vimochana	Burn unit, Victoria Hospital, Bengaluru	Social workers from Vimochana	Counselling and legal services to burn victims	Counsellors provide legal, police, and counselling support	Vimochana	Counselling services, advocacy for improving medical care for burn victims
SNEHA	Three medical colleges in Mumbai	Social workers from SNEHA	DV and rape referral for legal and social services	Identification by HPs, NGOs	SNEHA	Training of HPs
SWATI	Medical college in Gujarat	Counsellors appointed by SWATI	DV referrals for other services	Identification by HPs	SWATI	Training of HPs
Anweshi	Link with medical college, Calicut	Social workers from Anweshi	DV and rape	Referrals to Anweshi counselling centre	Anweshi	Sensitisation of staff and awareness of services provided by Anweshi
SECONDARY HOSPITALS/DISTRICT HOSPITAL						
Dilaasa	Eleven peripheral hospitals in Mumbai	Social workers deputed to the centre or hired for the centre	DV and rape medical, police, legal, and social support through strong referral mechanisms	Identification by HPs, self-referrals, police, NGOs	National Health Mission, Ministry of Health	Training of health professionals, police, and counsellors
Bhoomika	21 centres across 21 district hospitals in Kerala	Social workers hired for the centre	Counselling for DV referral to state legal aid for legal services	Self-referrals, identification by health providers	National Rural Health Mission, Ministry of Health	Training of HPs, district-level committees for intersectoral coordination

Iohlynti	Based in Shillong Civil Hospital	Deputation of social worker from Department of Social Welfare	Psycho-social support, police aid, referral to protection officer and legal aid, emergency shelter	Identification by HPs, NGOs, self-referral	Department of Women & Child Development, National Rural Health Mission	Training of HPs, training of police personnel
Sukoon	Four centres in district hospitals, Panchkula, Ambala, Yamuna Nagar, Panipat	Health resource centre	Psycho-social support, links with police stations and protection officers	Identification by HPs, self-referral	National Rural Health Mission and Directorate of Health Services	Training of hospital staff
Women's Crisis Centre	One crisis centre in North Goa district hospital, plans for one crisis centre in South Goa district hospital	Supported by NMEW and Directorate of Health Services	Psycho-social support; linkages with protection officer, legal aid, emergency shelter services	Identification by HPs, self-referral	NMEW, state Department of Women & Child Development	Training of HPs at hospitals and community health centres, awareness programmes in communities
PRIMARY LEVEL						
Soukhya	Maternity hospitals, doctors, ANMs, and community workers, Bengaluru	Staff deputed for the project, counsellors hired under the project	Counsellor on call for provision of crisis intervention services, referrals and links established for all services	Identification by HPs, awareness about forms of violence by community workers	Indian Council of Medical Research	Training, research
SWATI	CHC, ASHAs, Gujarat	Staff appointed by SWATI	Services at CHCs, community awareness and referral by ASHAs	Identification by HPs, awareness by ASHAs	SWATI	Training of HPs, front-line health workers; counselling services

Source: Role of health sector in addressing intimate partner violence in India: A synthesis report, International Center for Research on Women (ICRW).

Note: ANMs = auxiliary nurse midwives; ASHAs = accredited social health activists; CHCs = community health centres; DV = domestic violence; HPs = healthcare providers; NMEW = National Mission for Empowerment of Women.

are identified by health providers and referred to counselling services. Other women approach the centres after reading IEC material on the association between violence and health and the services available within the health facility.

What do the different models tell us?

These models have largely been initiated by CSOs, and a few by the state under its national health programme, the National Health Mission (NHM). The models cut across different levels of the health system – primary, secondary, and tertiary – in rural and urban areas. At the primary level, maternity homes, ASHAs, ANMs, and health workers have been sensitised; at the secondary level, the work has focused on rural hospitals and peripheral hospitals; and at the tertiary level, teaching hospitals have been addressing violence. The CSOs here include research institutions, feminist groups, and health researchers who have worked on the issue of VAW with the health sector. These efforts began in 1998, long before the Nirbhaya incident of 2012 brought people out in the streets demanding action on VAW.

To reiterate the main points of these models:

- All these models provide services to survivors of domestic violence, rape, and child sexual abuse (CSA).
- The services are survivor-centric counselling, with close coordination and formal links with protection officers, legal aid services, police, shelters, and so on.
- These models train healthcare providers to identify violence by understanding its signs and symptoms, provide medico-legal care and basic psychological support, and ensure procedures for private consultations and confidentiality of records. An important feature has been the setting up of core groups of health providers who take responsibility for the model. Almost all the models have a nodal officer at the hospital who liaises with other hospital departments for smooth and coordinated health services to survivors.
- CSOs have also painstakingly carried out process documentation of these models along with data analysis and monitoring of their work. IEC material has been developed to increase awareness about services at the hospitals where the models operate.
- Most CSOs have carried out advocacy with the local and state health system to encourage uptake of these models across different levels of the health system.

A large number of women access the services at all the initiatives operating within health facilities, pointing to the high acceptability of such services. Women's narratives reveal that this is the first place where they disclose violence. Women from the lower socioeconomic classes tend to access health facilities in the public sector, and so these services are available to the most marginalised population. The models provide a strong evidence base for developing a systematic health system response to VAW in India. The models located at the secondary level have been institutionalised and are funded through current health budgets. The other models are being operated through partnerships between the CSO and the health facility.

The rape crisis centres (RCCs) initiated by the Delhi state government and set up in a few of its hospitals, such as Ram Manohar Lohia and Safdarjung Hospitals, are different from the other models. In this case, the hospitals have merely assigned a separate room for examination and collection of medical evidence in cases of rape, while comprehensive services such as counselling support, shelter services, and referrals to legal aid are conspicuously absent. If survivors express other needs, they are directed to the Delhi Commission for Women for counselling. The existing team of counsellors and psychologists at these hospitals has no role at the hospital RCCs (CBGA and Jagori 2017). Such piecemeal approaches are neither helpful for survivors nor evidence-based.

Interventions to address violence against women in other sectors

The Ministry of Women and Child Development (MWCD) has also made several efforts to establish services for survivors of VAW/G. The MWCD has been responsible for establishing and running services such as Family Counselling Centres and Swadhar Grehs, or shelter homes, amongst others. Two other important models have been initiated: the special cell for women and children, initiated by the Tata Institute of Social Sciences (TISS) in the 1980s, and the aforementioned rape crisis centres, initiated by the Delhi Commission for Women (DCW).

Crisis centres located within police stations

In Mumbai, special cells for women and children are located at police stations. They were set up to enable women to benefit from law reforms such as Section 498A, which protects women against cruelty by marital families and harassment pertaining to dowry demands. The special cell counsels women at the level of police stations and helps facilitate police procedures. An important part of its work is sensitising police personnel to the issue of VAW and enabling comprehensive services at police stations. Another important component of the special cell's work is making home visits to assess the situation of the woman and carry out joint meetings with perpetrators. The special cell workers are expected to coordinate with women and visit the civil and criminal courts to assist them with legal proceedings.

The special cell began in 1984 in one police station of Mumbai as a joint project of TISS and the Mumbai police. By 1994, it was replicated in two additional police stations in Mumbai. In 2001, the Government of

Maharashtra entered into a formal collaboration with TISS Mumbai and the United Nations Development Fund for Women (UNIFEM) to set up the special cell in seven districts of Maharashtra. At the end of the contract period, the state Department of Women & Child Welfare took over the special cell programme and replicated it in 16 districts of Maharashtra. Between 2009 and 2013, the special cell was extended to other states, including Delhi, Odisha, Gujarat, Haryana, Madhya Pradesh, Andhra Pradesh, and Rajasthan. Different agencies have set up the special cells in each of these states – some by the state and some by NGOs. Special cells operating in different states, either with the support of NGOs or the MWCD, have not yet sought the one-stop centre (OSC) funds for cells in the police station (Dave 2014). MWCD started the OSC scheme under the Nirbhaya Fund, a separate fund created by the Government of India to respond holistically to VAW/G.

Rape crisis centre at the Delhi Commission for Women

Since 2005, the Delhi Commission for Women's rape crisis cell programme has been providing legal assistance in cases of sexual assault through collaboration with crisis intervention centres in each of its districts. The management of the crisis intervention centres (CICs) is outsourced to NGOs. After a case of rape or sexual assault is reported, the concerned investigation officer or station house officer (SHO) must inform a CIC counsellor. The CIC counsellor arrives at the police station and conducts all immediate crisis-response activities, such as counselling of the victim, informing her of her legal rights, and helping her with procedures to be followed, including the medico-legal certificate (MLC) examination. The RCC lawyer provides legal assistance and support to the victims of sexual assault in court, opposing bail applications of the accused and moving applications seeking victim compensation. The programme regularly takes up cases of extreme brutality, violation, and inaction of authorities (police or hospitals). The RCCs are funded through the state Department of Women & Child Development and central Social Welfare Board.

There is no information on recognition of RCCs as OSCs under the MWCD scheme, and neither has the Delhi Commission sought funds from MWCD to support RCCs.

One-stop centre (Sakhi) scheme by MCWD

The OSC scheme set up by the MWCD under Nirbhaya Funds envisaged making all services – medical care, counselling, police assistance, legal aid, and rehabilitation – available at a single place. While some of these OSCs are located within the premises of public hospitals, others are standalone OSCs that operate from existing MWCD infrastructure or separate buildings developed for OSCs. Many of these OSCs do not have collaborations or partnerships with hospitals, police stations, or courts, and hence their reach may be limited.

COURT-BASED ONE-STOP CRISIS CENTRE

Support during and after an investigation is necessary to facilitate the best psychological and medical treatment of women and girls surviving crimes. It is therefore important to have support services at the level of the court. It is a known fact that there is a complete absence of support for women in understanding and navigating court procedures. This necessitates the establishment of court-based OSCCs to assist the survivor of VAW from investigation to completion of trial. The OSCC helps with disbursal of compensation and witness protection. It works in close coordination with the public prosecutor and provides counsellors to accompany the survivor to the courts. The counsellors and lawyer assigned to the survivor keep abreast of court proceedings and communicate the progress of the case to the survivor from time to time.

Such an OSCC was set up by the Delhi State Legal Services Authority (DLSA) and has been functional since March 31, 2016, with one judicial assistant and one orderly posted at the centre. Counsellors sit for a few hours on weekends or come in when the centre has prior notice of a victim attending. The centre is primarily used for the recording of statements of minors and victims of sexual offences by magistrates under Section 164, Code of Criminal Procedure (CrPC).

The discussion has described the different approaches and efforts required to respond to the multiple needs of VAW/G survivors. Very few such approaches in India have been evaluated so far, and this volume attempts to bring together some promising approaches by CSOs as well as state governments. The next few sections of this volume underline the lessons learnt from (i) the institutionalised health system response to VAW, (ii) state-NGO collaborations to provide services to survivors, (iii) primary healthcare approaches at the community level to respond to and prevent VAW/G, and (iv) advocacy efforts demanding health sector accountability. We hope that policymakers, CSOs, and health providers can learn from these approaches and build on them to create an effective health system approach at all levels of service delivery.

References

Abrahams, N et al. (2014): "Worldwide prevalence of non-partner sexual violence: A systematic review," *The Lancet*, Vol 383, No 9929, pp. 1648–1654.

Agnes, F (2005): "To whom do experts testify?" Review of forensic textbooks," *Economic & Political Weekly*, Vol 40, No 18.

Arora, S, Bhate-Deosthali, P and Rege, S (2018): *Responding to domestic violence for improving maternal health outcomes: An evaluation of a counselling intervention for pregnant women in Mumbai*, Mumbai: Centre for Enquiry into Health and Allied Themes (CEHAT).

Bhate-Deosthali, P (2013): "Moving from evidence to care: Ethical responsibility of health professionals in responding to sexual assault," *Indian Journal of Medical Ethics*, Vol 10, No 1, pp. 2–5.

Bhate-Deosthali, P et al. (2018): *Role of health sector in addressing intimate partner violence in India: A synthesis report*, New Delhi: International Center for Research on Women (ICRW).

Bhate-Deosthali, P, Maghnani, P and Malik, S (2005): *Establishing Dilaasa: Documenting the challenges*, Mumbai: Centre for Enquiry into Health and Allied Themes (CEHAT).

Bhate-Deosthali, P, Ravindran, T K S and Vindhya, U (2012): "Addressing domestic violence within healthcare settings: The Dilaasa model," *Review of Women's Studies, Economic & Political Weekly*, Vol 47, No 17, pp. 66–75.

Bhate-Deosthali, P and Rege, S (2012): "Violence faced by women health workers," in *Sexual harassment at workplace*, D Deshpande and N Bhagwat (eds.), Nashik: Home Science Faculty of Gokhale Education Society's SMRK-BK-Mahila Mahavidyalaya, pp. 104–112.

Bott, S, Morrison, A and Ellsberg, M (2005): "Preventing and responding to gender-based violence in middle and low-income countries: A global review and analysis," Policy Research Working Paper 3618, World Bank.

CBGA and Jagori (2017): *Safety of women in public spaces in Delhi: Governance and budgetary challenges*, New Delhi: Centre for Budget and Governance Accountability and Jagori.

CEHAT-MCGM (2018): *Understanding dynamics of sexual violence: Study of case records*, Mumbai: Centre for Enquiry into Health and Allied Themes and Municipal Corporation of Greater Mumbai.

Dave, A (2014): *Women survivors of violence: Genesis and growth of a state support system*, New Delhi: Orient Black Swan.

Garcia-Moreno, C M et al. (2014): "Addressing violence against women: A call to action," *The Lancet*, Vol 385, No 9978, pp. 1685–1695.

Garcia-Moreno, C M et al. (2015): "The health-systems response to violence against women," *The Lancet*, Vol 385, No 9977, pp. 1567–1579.

Government of India (2005): *The protection of women from domestic violence act, 2005*, New Delhi: Department of Law & Justice, Government of India.

Government of India (2012): *The protection of children from sexual offences act 2012*, New Delhi: Department of Law & Justice, Government of India.

Government of India (2013): *Criminal law (Amendment) act (2013)*, New Delhi: Department of Law & Justice, Government of India.

Gupte, M (2013): "Why feminism should inform our routine interventions in domestic violence," in *Feminist counselling and domestic violence in India*, P Bhate-Deosthali, S Rege and P Prakash (eds.), Centre for Enquiry into Health and Allied Themes (CEHAT), Mumbai: Routledge, pp. 20–48.

Hameed, S S (2005): "Testimony of Shah Bano: Sexual abuse in revenge: Women as targets of communal hatred," in *The violence of normal times: Essays of women's lived realities*, K Kannabiran (ed.), New Delhi: Women Unlimited in Association with Kali for Women, p. 317.

Heise, L, Ellsberg, M and Gottemoeller, M (1999): *Ending violence against women*, Population Reports Series L, No 11, Baltimore: John Hopkins University School of Public Health, Population Information Program.

HRW (2016): *Bound by brotherhood: India's failure to end killings in police custody*, Human Rights Watch, United states of America.

International Institute for Population Sciences (IIPS) and ICF (2017): *National Family Health Survey (NFHS-4), 2015–16: India*, Mumbai: IIPS.

International Institute for Population Sciences (IIPS) and Macro International (2007): *National Family Health Survey (NFHS-3), 2005–06: India: Volume I*, Mumbai: IIPS.

Jaising, I (2014): "Concern for the dead, condemnation for the living," *Economic & Political Weekly*, Vol 49, No 30.

Jejeebhoy, J S (1998): "Wife beating in rural India: A husband's right? Evidence from survey data," *Economic & Political Weekly*, Vol 33, No 15.

Jewkes, R et al. (2002): Chapter 6, "Sexual violence," in *World report on violence and health*, Geneva: World Health Organization, pp. 149–181.

JVC Report (2013): *Report of committee on amendments to criminal law*, J S Verma, L Seth and G Subramanium (eds.), Chapter 11, New Delhi: Rajya Sabha Secretariat.

Kalokhe, A S et al. (2015): "How well does the World Health Organization definition of domestic violence work for India?," *PLoS One*, Vol 10, No 3.

Khanday, Z (2017): "Exploring religious discrimination toward women in public health facilities in Mumbai," *Social Sciences*, Vol 6, No 6, pp. 148–159.

Khot, A, Menon, S and Dilip, T (2004): *Domestic violence: Levels, correlates, causes, impact, and response: A community-based study of married women from Mumbai slums*, Mumbai: Centre for Enquiry into Health and Allied Themes (CEHAT).

Krishnan, S (2005): "Gender, caste, and economic inequalities and marital violence in rural South India," *Health Care for Women International*, Vol 26, No 1, pp. 87–99.

Kumar, R (1993): *The history of doing: An illustrated account of movements for women's rights and feminism in India, 1800–1990*, New Delhi: Zubaan.

Mahajan, A (1990): "Instigators of wife battering," in *Violence against women*, S Sood (ed.), Jaipur: Arihant Publisher, pp. 1–10.

MFC (2002): *Medico friend circle bulletin*, editorial, July–August, Vadodara: Medico Friend Circle.

Michau, L et al. (2015): "Prevention of violence against women and girls: Lessons from practice," *The Lancet*, Vol 385, No 9978, pp. 1672–1684.

MoHFW (2014): *Guidelines and protocols: Medico-legal care for survivors/victims of sexual violence*, Ministry of Health and Family Welfare, Government of India.

MoHFW (2017): *National health policy*, Ministry of Health and Family Welfare, Government of India.

NCRB (2014): *Crime in India 2014: Statistics*, New Delhi: National Crime Records Bureau, Ministry of Home Affairs, Government of India.

NCRB (2015): *Crime in India 2015: Statistics*, New Delhi: National Crime Records Bureau, Ministry of Home Affairs, Government of India.

NCRB (2016): *Crime in India 2016: Statistics*, New Delhi: National Crime Records Bureau, Ministry of Home Affairs, Government of India.

Pande, R P et al. (2017): *Addressing intimate partner violence in South Asia: Evidence for interventions in the health sector, women's collectives, and local governance mechanisms*, New Delhi: International Centre for Research on Women, p. 10.

Rao, V (1997): "Wife-beating in rural South India: A qualitative and econometric analysis," *Social Science & Medicine*, Vol 44, No 8, pp. 1169–1180.

Rege, S and Bhate-Deosthali, P (2018): "Violence against women as a health care issue: Perceptions and approaches," in *Equity and access: Healthcare studies in India*, P Prasad and A Jesani (eds.), Oxford: Oxford University Press, pp. 287–302.

Santhya, K G and Jejeebhoy, J S (2007): "Early marriage and HIV/AIDS," *Economic & Political Weekly*, Vol 42, No 14.

Solotaroff, J L and Pande, R P (2014): *Violence against women and girls: Lessons from South Asia*, Washington, DC: South Asia Development Forum, World Bank.

Stöckl, H et al. (2013): "The global prevalence of intimate partner homicide: A systematic review," *The Lancet*, Vol 382, No 9895, pp. 859–865.

UN (1993): "Declaration on the elimination of violence against women," General Assembly Resolution 48/104 of December 20, 1993, United Nations.

UNDP (2015): *Sustainable development goals*, United Nations Development Programme.

UNICEF (2014): *A statistical snapshot of violence against adolescent girls*, New York: United Nations Children's Fund.

UN OHCHR (1992): "General recommendation 19: Violence against women," adopted by the Committee on the Elimination of Discrimination Against Women, Office of the High Commissioner on Human Rights, United Nations.

Varma D et al. (2007): "Intimate partner violence and sexual coercion among pregnant women in India: Relationship with depression and post-traumatic stress disorder," *Journal of Affective Disorders*, Vol 102, No 1–3, pp. 227–235.

Visaria, L (2000): "Violence against women: A field study," *Economic and Political Weekly*, Vol 35, No 20, pp. 1742–1751.

WHO (2013a): *Global and regional estimates of violence against women: Prevalence and health effects of intimate partner violence and non-partner sexual violence*, Geneva: World Health Organization.

WHO (2013b): *Responding to intimate partner violence and sexual violence against women: WHO clinical and policy guidelines*, Geneva: World Health Organization.

WHO (2016): *Violence against women (fact sheet no 239)*, Geneva: World Health Organization.

Williamson, E (2013): "Measuring gender-based violence: Issues of impact and prevalence," in *Gender-based violence and public health*, K Nakray (ed.), Abingdon, UK: Routledge, pp. 65–78.

World Health Assembly (1996): *Prevention of violence: Public health priority*, Geneva: World Health Organization.

Section 2

Institutionalising a health system response

Introduction

The case studies presented in this section represent interventions on violence against women that are staffed, managed, and financed by health systems and thus have maximum integration with the public health system. This is in contrast to the interventions that follow in Section 3 of this volume, which are partnerships between health systems and civil society organisations, where CSOs are providing direct services to survivors of VAW within public health facilities.

The interventions in this section emerge from CEHAT's Dilaasa hospital-based model in response to VAW. CEHAT's engagement with the states of Meghalaya, Kerala, and Haryana, with the help of CSOs such as the North East Network (NEN) and feminist activists in Kerala and Haryana, provided the impetus to establish these health system responses to violence against women.

The North East Network's Iohlynti hospital-based crisis centre traces its genesis to 2003, when the health sector had not yet recognised VAW as a health issue. NEN is a feminist organisation working on human rights.

The popular conception is that women in Northeast India enjoy equality with men and do not face discrimination and violence. However, NEN's surveys and studies have established that this is a misconception. Even matrilineal societies are not free of domestic violence. In the course of their work with women, NEN recognised that women had no autonomy over their reproductive health and that control often lay with their spouse. NEN carried out several orientations and trainings of women in urban and rural areas to raise awareness of the links between violence and reproductive health. They entered the formal health system with the conviction that VAW is a health issue. In 2007, NEN entered into a collaboration with the state health department to set up a hospital-based crisis centre. Their case study explains how NEN used data from hospital records to determine the facility prevalence of VAW. Slowly and steadily, they got the opportunity to build the capacities of healthcare providers, who eventually started identifying the signs and symptoms of VAW and referring these women to the centre.

Having established the hospital-based crisis centre, NEN's next goal was to institutionalise it by advocating for the deputation of government counsellors to the centre, ensuring that it became a hospital entity. They were able to establish a multi-sectoral response with the deputation of a counsellor from the social welfare department. Their case study presents useful lessons on how to engage with state departments to institutionalise a response to VAW.

The Bhoomika centres established by Kerala, the Sukoon centres by Haryana, and Dilaasa centres in Mumbai, Maharashtra, are government efforts to set up crisis counselling services for women and children facing violence. Kerala was one of the first states to initiate gender budgeting and to design and implement a health system response to VAW. Haryana had a feminist gender consultant engaged with the women's health movement who raised concerns around non-recognition of VAW as a public health issue and then facilitated the setting up of centres. Mumbai, by contrast, was a response to the effectiveness of Dilaasa and aimed to replicate it across states. The union health secretary recommended the upscaling of the Dilaasa model.

The Bhoomika crisis centres were set up in 14 districts, each at a district hospital. The Kerala State Planning Board (KSPB) allocated Rs 50 lakh in 2008–09 to the health department to set up a special programme for addressing domestic violence. In the initial stages (2010), a single counsellor was expected to provide all services to women, but recognising the high caseload, the number was increased in 2014 to two counsellors. Counsellors were equipped to provide crisis intervention services and liaise with shelter homes and legal aid services. However, the nature of support received from hospitals in the initial stages was limited. Health providers did not see violence as a health issue, and if they did, they saw it as an illness to be treated with medication. Anything beyond the physical ailment was considered beyond their scope. This necessitated the training of health providers, and these trainings were to be conducted by experts who would command the respect of doctors and nurses. A hospital institutional committee governs the Bhoomika centres. The committee comprises heads of departments, such as gynaecology, surgery, and paediatrics, and a district-level committee comprising NRHM officials, hospital officials, members of the police, legal aid personnel, protection officers, and NGO representatives. The Bhoomika case study presents the Kerala government's step-by-step approach in setting up the services and the governing mechanisms for the centre.

The Haryana state health resource department set up the Sukoon centres in 2013–14. The principal secretary (health) took a keen interest in setting them up, as they were seen as a legal requirement after the Nirbhaya case in Delhi. The Sukoon case study documents the efforts made to quantify the number of cases of VAW reaching hospitals. An analysis of the hospital's medico-legal records found that many women reporting to the emergency department were reporting the consequences of violence. In the initial phases, the hospital counsellors were expected to respond to VAW, but they did not have the required training and also had existing responsibilities. Assessing these constraints, efforts were made to integrate the personnel and infrastructure requirements into the NRHM budgets. The Sukoon case study presents the public health system's attempts to establish crisis intervention services, appoint doctors as nodal officers, and ensure mainstreaming of violence as a health issue.

The replication of the Dilaasa crisis centres by the Mumbai Mahanagar Palika with a dedicated budget in the NHM represents recognition of the success of the Dilaasa crisis centre established in 2000. The budget provided for recruitment of a team comprising two counsellors, two auxiliary nurse midwives, and a data entry operator. This indicated the understanding that the appointment of a single counsellor does not constitute a crisis centre. The replicated Dilaasa centres have a core group of doctors and nurses to support the Dilaasa team if they encounter challenges. The core group is also responsible for mainstreaming the VAW response through orientation trainings and meetings. Having a core group from the hospital enables Dilaasa centres to become a hospital department run as part of hospital services.

The Dilaasa case study presents the process of equipping healthcare providers with the knowledge and skills to run the hospital-based crisis centres as well as the process of building a feminist perspective in the response of counsellors to VAW. An important component of the Dilaasa crisis centres is the management information system (MIS) that records data on the number of women identified with health consequences, their profile, and the nature of support sought by them. The case study highlights the importance of linkages outside of the hospital to create support for women facing violence. These range from links to protection officers and police stations to skill-building and income-generation opportunities.

The four case studies indicate that there has been a progressive understanding and recognition of violence against women as a health issue by formal health systems. These models represent an institutionalised system as opposed to an NGO-dependent one, where the health system commits resources to VAW and ensures accountability from them. All these models are aimed at the health system's response to domestic violence and sexual violence. All of them began with a response to domestic violence and then included a response to survivors of sexual violence. The government funds all of them, and all of them were inspired by the Dilaasa model.

Dilaasa and Bhoomika have set up committees to monitor their models. Only the Dilaasa centres in Mumbai are ensuring gender-sensitive care for sexual violence. Meghalaya and Maharashtra have adopted the MoHFW medico-legal guidelines of 2014, but Kerala and Haryana have not. While Meghalaya has initiated a health system response as part of an intersectoral response to VAW led by NEN, the other three are purely responses from the health system under NRHM and NHM.

Bhoomika, Sukoon, and Iohlynti are replications of Dilaasa, and the Mumbai centres are an upscaling of the Dilaasa crisis centre first introduced at a single hospital in 2000. All of them receive approximately 200–300 survivors per year, depending on the size of the hospital. As there is little evidence regarding the health complaints and pathways to the crisis intervention centres, it is difficult to pinpoint the nature of abuse, but it may be safe to say that overt signs such as assaults, poisoning, and rape are being picked up. As of now, there is no evidence regarding the medicalisation of violence and no reporting on mandatory referrals for mental health services. What we do have is a recognition of the multiple needs of survivors and an understanding of domestic violence as a public health issue and not a disease.

2.1 North East Network (NEN)

Darilyn Syiem

The Iohlynti crisis centre at a women's hospital in Shillong is the first psychological and social support centre in the Northeast for women experiencing violence.

Northeast India is a land-locked region connected to the rest of the country by a thin strip of land commonly known as the chicken's neck.

> Although the region shares several common features such as terrain, racial characteristics, absence of caste systems, village systems based on familial ties and methods of cultivation, it is . . . not a homogenous [sic] unit. The region is home to several diverse tribal and ethnic groups and sub-groups. Each group is keenly aware of its ethnicity and fiercely guards and asserts [its] ethnicity with passion and fervour. The hopes, aspirations, ethnic loyalties and reticent nature of the people have been little understood by the Indian State and this has led to a deep sense of alienation in the region.
>
> (Goswami, Sreekala, and Goswami 2005)

These conflicting identities have led to years of armed conflict between the state and various ethnic groups and between one ethnic group and another. Though there is no overt conflict at present, the low-intensity, protracted conflict could lead to sudden outbreaks of violence, as in July 2012, when riots between the indigenous Bodos and Bengali-speaking Muslims broke out, many people died, thousands became homeless, and several went missing.

> The impact of all of this on women and girls has been especially devastating, debilitating and far-reaching. Sexual violence, displacement and loss of support bases, disappearances and extra-judicial killings of family members, lack of all forms of human security and [a] constant sense of fear and dread are some of the more obvious fallout[s], while the culture of impunity and corruption that has seeped into the very fabric of their

existence undermines the basic dignity of women and girls and impedes gender equality and gender justice.

(NAWO 2014)

The North East Network (NEN), with its strong feminist and human rights perspective, has been addressing a range of women's rights issues in the Northeast. The organisation adopts an intersectional approach to various forms of rights violations and discrimination and works within the CEDAW framework of equality, non-discrimination, and state obligation for the realisation of women's human rights. NEN has been at the forefront of work on violence against women in a region where women are believed to enjoy greater mobility and visibility than women elsewhere in India. Women in Meghalaya, however, do not live in an ideal world. "Even in a matrilineal society, homes are not free of domestic violence, with consequential effects on women and children" (Government of Meghalaya 2008: 194). In 2013 and 2014, the total number of crimes against women was 336 and 343, respectively (Meghalaya Police 2014), and the state recorded the highest number of domestic violence cases in the region (NFHS-2 1998–99).

The issue of health became important to NEN in the course of its work because health is critical in a conflict-hit region. NEN's surveys have shown the dismal position of public health services in rural areas. Poor road connectivity exists between urban and rural areas. This further compounds access to health care for poor residing in rural areas. It is imperative for them to access public health services. Reproductive and general healthcare became the focus of NEN's training and dissemination. The main objective was to move from the needs perspective to the rights perspective in healthcare for women. While working on women's reproductive health and rights, NEN realised that intimate partner violence is a major cause of women's ill health and no amount of healthcare interventions can ensure the well-being of women unless this is addressed.

In 1997, for instance, during a training session on reproductive healthcare in the village of Mawkaphan, all the women and men said that the number of children they have depends on the "will of God." Later that evening, during a conversation with the woman at whose house we were staying, we posed the question of the number of children again. Her response was the same, and when we asked if her children were in school, she replied that the elder ones had to discontinue schooling to help in the fields and look after their younger siblings. To this, we responded, "Do you think it is the will of God that your children remain illiterate?" "Of course not," she replied, "but what can I do? I have to give in, especially when my husband comes home after a drink or two. If I resist, it may turn nasty, and the neighbours will hear."

For several years, NEN worked independently, but eventually the organisation felt the need to link with state agencies and make them responsible for implementing policies that promote women's access to rights. At the time, however, the government took little notice of NGOs, and it was only when

NEN started working with the agriculture department in Meghalaya in 2003 that they voiced the possibility of collaboration. Emboldened by the positive response, in 2007 NEN introduced a project on violence against women in collaboration with the state health system. CEHAT played a major role in helping NEN convince the health department that VAW is a public health issue and responsibility. The long-term objective of the project is to advocate for a strengthened healthcare response to VAW and to institutionalise VAW as a state public health concern.

Approaches to working with the health system

NEN's strategies include networking, alliance-building, training and capacity-building, national and international advocacy, research, and documentation. In its work with the health system in Meghalaya, NEN's approach has been to build partnerships between women's rights groups and state agencies, where the former is able to influence mindsets and behaviour and build the capacities of the state agencies in dealing with cases of VAW.

Initial research on how healthcare providers treat cases of VAW in public hospitals in Shillong, the capital of Meghalaya, revealed that doctors had little understanding of VAW and were ill-equipped or too overworked to deal with such cases beyond the diagnostic and prescriptive boundaries. In an interview, a very senior doctor, who was also the nodal officer appointed by the health department for the collaborative work on VAW, said,

> Our duty is to accept cases, whether they are due to illness or injuries. The system to accept these cases of VAW exists, but it is not very systematic. . . . We do not have the system to treat cases of violence against women in the right perspective and we do not have counselling centres or crisis centres to help women who are abused.

During the research, doctors and nurses admitted that they provided the necessary clinical help but felt their duty did not extend beyond this. Even if they wanted to, they did not know how to go about it. However, they felt strongly that emotional help and support services are essential for abused women.

This big gap in services is a setback for women who want to share more than their medical problems. NEN set out to fill this gap through capacity-building of healthcare providers and the creation of a support centre for women within the Ganesh Das Hospital for Women and Children in Shillong. Simultaneously, NEN continued to strengthen its alliance with line agencies within the state, including the police, social welfare department, state legal services authority, and state women's commission, as well as traditional women's groups and NGOs. The idea was to design a strong and reliable referral service to which identified survivors have free and easy access.

NEN also used "opportunistic persistence" as a key strategy to influence policymakers in the health department. This term refers to the "skills of communication, knowledge of the sociocultural environment and wit to navigate and persist against difficult odds" (Gurung, Syiem, and Gurung 2010).

Key components of the model

NEN's research and observation revealed that an abused woman admitted to hospital is treated for her bodily wounds and nothing more. On one occasion, NEN members met a patient from Sohryngkham village whose head had been hacked by her husband. As we talked to her, we sensed that the woman wanted to tell us more but could not because of her critical condition. It was obvious that she needed someone to listen to her pain and trauma. The doctors at the hospital had no time to converse with an abused woman, though this would have made a lot of difference to her overall recovery. To address this, NEN decided to facilitate a deeper understanding of violence against women amongst doctors and nurses.

Separate two- and three-day trainings on gender-sensitisation and information-sharing on violence against women were conducted for the doctors, nurses, counsellors, health educators, and other support staff at the Ganesh Das Hospital. These included training of trainers who would act as change agents within the government. Initially, CEHAT facilitated these trainings, and now NEN continues them, using some of the trained doctors as trainers for some sessions.

The trainings aimed to enable healthcare providers to:

- Understand violence against women and why violence is a public health issue
- Understand the role of healthcare providers in dealing with VAW cases
- Identify cases of VAW and refer them to crisis centres for women for non-clinical support services

The training and methodology follow the CEHAT module, covering an understanding of gender and violence against women, the role of healthcare providers, and the concept of feminist counselling.

The trainings have enhanced the quality of the institutional response to VAW. Between 2008 and 2014, NEN trained 215 healthcare providers, including nurses, support staff, doctors, community health workers, health educators, and health counsellors. Some of the trained doctors have used the MoHFW guidelines for medico-legal care when dealing with sexual violence and have encouraged their colleagues to use them as well. There has been an amazing response from doctors: one very senior gynaecologist felt that the gender-sensitisation training has helped her listen to her patients and see how certain complaints and symptoms are linked to violence. The gynaecologist had a case where the victim of violence did not want to go to the protection officer, but she was able to make the woman aware of the PWDV Act herself.

The doctor has also shared what she learned in the training and during her association with the project team with her colleagues.

These small successes that followed from NEN's persistent efforts resulted in the setting up of Iohlynti (meaning "find a way"), a support centre for women, in November 2011, at the Civil Hospital, Shillong. This was the outcome of a convergence meeting of the government's line agencies on a public policy response to violence against women and the commitment by the then principal secretary, health department, to provide full support for counselling facilities for women survivors of violence. The centre is the first of its kind in the Northeast and the only one in the region to date. Situating this service centre at a hospital enables women victims of domestic violence to access psychological and social support safely, without increasing their vulnerability and without any restrictions or suspicion, for here, as much as elsewhere in India, a culture of silence and shame surrounds VAW. Iohlynti provides trauma counselling services, free legal aid, guidance, and referrals. The health department has now allotted a separate space for Iohlynti at the Ganesh Das Hospital for Women and Children in Shillong because the one at the Civil Hospital was a temporary space and because most sexual assault cases come to the women's hospital. At present, doctors are referring cases not only from the two public hospitals in Shillong but also from civil hospitals and community health centres in other districts of the state.

From November 2011 to January 2015, Iohlynti received 153 cases of domestic violence, sexual assault, attempted suicide, and substance abuse. The greatest number of cases for women from the 21–40 age group involved domestic violence. As many as 64.03% of the cases are single mothers. As in the rest of the country, the number of single mothers is increasing, the reasons for which we will not go into here except to state that in matrilineal Meghalaya, cohabitation with a man of the woman's choice is acceptable. Though cohabitation is not an issue in this society, it

> becomes a problem when the man abandons his wife. Matriliny makes it incumbent upon the woman to bring up her children on her own. More often than not, women find it hard to claim maintenance for themselves and their children. Often, even if the courts decree that the man is to pay a part of his salary to the woman he has abandoned, he hardly does that.
>
> (Mukhim 2010)

As mentioned earlier, a network of agencies (legal aid services, state commission for women, and others) within the government, which are responsible for the safety and security of women and children, had been set up before Iohlynti was created. These agencies have been trained to identify cases of violence that they encounter and to refer them to the Iohlynti support centre for women created within the health system. This network is a lifeline for survivors who want to take their cases beyond counselling – that is, seek legal help or file their cases in court. The Iohlynti support centre refers cases to the Meghalaya State Legal Services Authority (MSLSA), which provides free legal aid to the poor. Women are referred to the police for the filing of cases in court, and the police are also trained and sensitised by NEN.

There are gaps in the functioning of the MSLSA because of the lack of gender sensitivity and familiarity in handling cases of violence. However, if a survivor who visits Iohlynti wants protection from domestic violence, her case is referred to the protection officer in her district. There have been cases where the abused woman wanted only acknowledgement from the man who had made her pregnant but refused to marry her. The thought of bringing a fatherless child into the world gives women a feeling of shame, and this is so in a matrilineal society as well. Such cases are referred to the State Commission for Women for settlement. Thus, NEN has formed a cadre of boundary partners on VAW through individuals, groups, organisations, and departments with whom the organisation's programme interacts directly to effect change and with whom the programme can anticipate some opportunities for influence (Earl, Carden, and Smutlyo 2001). Boundary partners can range from local communities, government officials, and the private sector to research and educational institutions.

Meanwhile, at the community level, NEN has been working to mitigate VAW with the women's groups in the dorbars (village councils). These local bodies are in charge of village administration, including the safety and security of its inhabitants. There have been instances when the dorbar has taken up cases of sexual violence and meted out what it considered justice. For example, some dorbars have resolved rape cases by making the perpetrator pay a certain amount of money to the victim. Communities take these decisions seriously. Given the power these local bodies have, NEN realised that it was important to gender-sensitise the dorbars. NEN therefore initiated the subcommittees on VAW as part of the dorbar system, with men and women as members. Over the last eight years, NEN has organised several awareness programmes and trainings on VAW and involved dorbar members in state and national consultations. This has given them a deeper understanding of VAW and a rights perspective. Local women facing domestic violence have approached these subcommittees to file FIRs in police stations and refer the cases requiring counselling to Iohlynti. The local dorbars also help publicise Iohlynti by making announcements through loudspeakers fixed at various points in the locality. Other NGOs that provide counselling services on alcoholism and drug addiction also refer cases to Iohlynti.

Reflections

Since its inception in 1995, NEN's work, from the grassroots to the policy level, has earned visibility and acknowledgement from the community and the state. The governments in all three states – Meghalaya, Assam, and

Nagaland – where the organisation works have set up partnerships with NEN, and this is perhaps a result of NEN's advocacy to highlight gender-based violence.

It is encouraging that the Meghalaya government now recognises NEN's work and invites its members to high-level consultations on crimes against women. NEN is simultaneously working with the police and law department in the state, which enables them to track coordination between these sectors, especially on sexual assault cases. NEN faced no difficulty or resistance in conducting surveys on sexual assault cases in hospitals and could get access to information regarding procedures followed in recording medico-legal cases. However, these surveys have raised another concern. They have shown that cases of sexual assault are examined cursorily using a one-page form attached to the consent form. All cases of sexual assault that come to other public hospitals are referred to the Ganesh Das Hospital for Women and Children. Moreover, doctors say that they usually provide only what the police ask for and not more for fear of the ramifications.

The allotment of a formal space within hospital premises for a support/crisis centre for women survivors of violence is an indicator of the policy response secured by NEN from Meghalaya's health sector. The fact that a temporary space was allotted immediately, followed by the official allotment of a permanent space for Iohlynti in September 2014, establishes that this is not tokenism on the part of the government, as has been the case when women's rights groups have asked for state commitment in the past.

Looking back, it would seem that the convergence meeting mentioned earlier, which encouraged the cross-fertilisation of ideas and inter-departmental collaboration on the issue of VAW, was an effective innovation by NEN. It provided a platform for NEN to draw out resolutions, the most critical being the commitment for a separate counselling space for women survivors of violence. The second equally strategic innovation has been the creation of boundary partners around the issue of VAW, for it is only when there is collective effort and responsibility that change can happen, transforming a victim into a survivor who has the ability to make effective choices and transform those choices into desired outcomes (World Bank 2012). The women who come to Iohlynti all want freedom from violence, and this is perhaps the most fundamental expression of women's agency.

Challenges

Despite the positive response of the health system in Meghalaya, there is still a lack of understanding – or maybe a denial – that violence against women is a consequence of structural inequalities and social processes. This is particularly true of the bureaucracy, and it results in delay of approvals for programmes and a disinclination to make financial commitments. In addition, NEN is apprehensive that "the narrowing of the analysis of sexual crimes to evidentiary, medical and legal aspects strips away the context of oppression" (TAL9000 2012). So far, medical interventions in domestic and sexual violence have accepted the need for "sensitivity" towards survivors and improvements in service delivery through identification and screening procedures. However, the focus is still not on justice and equality. Such attitudes may swallow up the early wins and send the social change work quietly into oblivion. It is therefore critical that while NEN intensifies the gender-sensitisation trainings, it also strengthens its advocacy efforts with the health department to ensure an institutionalised response to violence against women – getting the department to sign the memorandum of understanding stating that Iohlynti is an integrated department of the hospital that it has shelved since 2011, for instance. It is heartening to know that the Ganesh Das Hospital in Shillong and the Civil Hospital in Jowai are following the sexual assault healthcare guidelines developed by the health ministry, but this has to be systematised and practiced in all public hospitals in the state. The health sector and the state as a whole are obliged to take proactive policy measures to curb violence against women and acknowledge it as a public health issue and a violation of women's human rights.

On another note, the Government of Meghalaya, through its social welfare department, has committed to appointing a full-time counsellor for Iohlynti, but this is still pending. NEN has tried to get the health department to provide the counsellor, but this responsibility was shifted to the social welfare department. This is disturbing, as it dilutes the essential meaning of violence as a public health issue, making it a welfare matter all over again. Despite all these years of engagement with the health department on domestic violence and sexual violence, they are not keen to take on the responsibility of service delivery for survivors. Infrastructural support has been made available, but a long-term investment in human resources needs to be made; otherwise, the sustainability of the support centre is at risk.

Recently, the social welfare department has planned to set up a Nirbhaya Centre on the premises of the Pasteur Institute, which is just next to the women's hospital where Iohlynti is located. The department assumes that Iohlynti will then function from this institute. NEN has suggested that Iohlynti be housed there when the Nirbhaya Centre is set up. Trauma cases can be registered and treated at the Nirbhaya Centre, which is the first-stage unit, and cases requiring counselling can be referred to Iohlynti, which is the second-stage unit. In this way, traumatised women can be saved the time and effort of moving from one building to another and being further traumatised. Meanwhile, cases referred by doctors for counselling can continue to be registered directly at Iohlynti. When such a set-up of support services for women facing violence is under one roof, it will showcase the convergence of two state departments, health and social welfare, and sustain the collaboration between the government and NEN. Perhaps it can be named the Nirbhaya-Iohlynti Centre (meaning "the fearless find a way"). However, NEN's concern is that two set-ups in the same facility would lead to an overlapping of services. These tensions will need to be resolved as the work proceeds. Importantly, NEN aims to ensure that the health department does not give up its responsibility to VAW.

References

Earl, S, Carden, F and Smutylo, T (2001): *Outcome mapping: Building learning and reflection into development programs*, Ottawa, Canada: International Development Research Centre.

Goswami, R, Sreekala, M G and Goswami, M (2005): *Women in armed conflict situations: A study by North East Network*, North East Network, Guwhati.

Government of Meghalaya (2008): *Meghalaya human development report 2008*, Shillong: Planning Department, Government of Meghalaya.

Gurung, B, Syiem, D and Gurung, N (2010): "Navigating bureaucratic narratives: Generating legitimacy and accountability for gender equality," *Gender, Technology and Development*, Vol 14, No 1, pp. 45–66.

Meghalaya Police (2014): "Month-wise distribution of crime reported against women in Meghalaya during the year 2014." www.megpolice.gov.in/sites/default/files/district_crime_2014.pdf

Mukhim, P (2010): "Break the gender myth," *The Telegraph*, March 9.

NAWO (2014): "Women in conflict prevention, conflict and post conflict situation," in *India's 4th and 5th NGO alternative report on CEDAW*, New Delhi, India: National Alliance of Women.

NFHS (1998–99): *National Family Health Survey-2 publications (1998–99)*, International Institute for Population Sciences (IIPS), and Ministry of Health and Family Welfare (MoHFW), Government of India, Mumbai.

TAL9000 (2012): "The medicalization of domestic violence," web log, *Tumblr*.

World Bank (2012): *World development report 2012: Gender equality and development*, Washington, DC: World Bank.

2.2 Bhoomika

V Jithesh

Kerala was the first state to recognise VAW as a public health priority. Its decade-old Bhoomika programme, in 21 district and taluka hospitals, was rooted in the public health system from the outset.

Introduction

Kerala is a state with some of the best social and health indicators in India: highest female literacy, lowest infant mortality, and lowest maternal mortality rate. It pioneered the women's empowerment scheme called Kudumbasree, a community-based self-help initiative for women that aims to alleviate poverty through micro-finance and micro-enterprises.

However, Kerala presents a paradox of sorts, with a relatively higher human development index and gender development index yet simultaneously poor participation of women in political and economic processes. Violence against women and sexual harassment have been increasing over the years. The INCLEN-ICRW study (2000) of domestic violence in India reported rates of physical violence as high as 43.1% in urban non-slum areas and up to 46% in rural areas of Thiruvananthapuram. The reported prevalence of psychological violence is 61.6% in urban non-slum areas and 68.6% in rural areas. The overall violence rates reported by the same study were 64% in urban non-slum areas and 71% in rural areas of the district (INCLEN-ICRW 2000). A study commissioned by the Government of Kerala and conducted by Sakhi Resource Centre for Women, Thiruvananthapuram (Vijayan 2004), revealed that 38.6% of women surveyed had experienced some form of violence, of which the most prevalent was physical violence (30%), followed by psychological abuse (21%), economic violence (17%), and sexual violence (5%). The same study reported that in the 12 months preceding the survey, 7.1% of women experienced physical violence, 7.3% economic violence, 6.8% psychological abuse, and 1.8% sexual violence.

In 2008–09, the Kerala State Planning Board (KSPB) decided to do a detailed analysis of the gender orientation of government schemes and programmes on the understanding that moving towards a more gender equitable society calls for proper planning, including gender-sensitive budgets. The gender budgeting handbook for Government of India ministries and departments defines a gender-responsive budget as "one that acknowledges the gender patterns in society and allocates money to implement policies and programmes that will change these patterns in a way that moves towards a more gender equal society." Kerala had already initiated the process of gender-responsive budgeting through panchayati raj institutions in 1998 by mandating that local self-governments should allocate at least 10% of their plan funds for women. However, the state budget began the gender budgeting process from only 2008–09, when the government reiterated the need to collect gender-disaggregated data and create mechanisms to ensure gender sensitivity in policies and programmes. A gender analysis of the 2008–09 budget by Mridul Eapen, member, State Planning Board for the Ministry of Women and Child Development, Government of India, revealed that, apart from the departments "traditionally" considered to be looking after women's affairs, hardly any department had specific programmes targeted at women (Vijayan and George 2010).

In the 11th Plan period, the Kerala state government planned to take up certain initiatives through gender-responsive flagship programmes, including gender awareness programmes and implementation of the PWDV Act. Therefore, besides instructing all government departments to consider gender budgeting in their programmes, KSPB specifically instructed the Department of Health to take the lead in addressing domestic and sexual violence against women. The reasons cited by the planning board for this specific direction to the health department were, firstly, that there is a strong link between domestic/sexual violence and various health issues of women and, secondly, that the first and safest point of contact for women who suffer from domestic and sexual violence is always the health system.

The KSPB allotted Rs 50 lakh in 2008–09 to the health department to set up a special programme to address domestic violence, with the specific clause that the fund should not lapse at the end of the financial year and should not be re-appropriated for any other activity. It is against this background that the health department of Kerala decided to take up a plan to respond to domestic violence in earnest.

Prevention or response: the dilemma

The initial concern for the health department was to zero in on the best health system response to GBV. Several consultations with different expert groups, including women's groups and health activists, followed. There were demands for two different approaches: preventive activities by women's groups and health sector activities by health activists. Finally, the department decided to begin with a system to respond to the needs of survivors of violence and later develop it to address the root causes of GBV. This decision was prompted by the following considerations:

1 The primary responsibility of the health system is to provide healthcare. Therefore, medical care, counselling support, and safety of women survivors of violence should take precedence over prevention efforts.
2 Managing the consequences of violence is itself a major preventive activity, as there is an opportunity to prevent further episodes of violence; it can act as a deterrent.
3 This system can act as a nucleus for community-based awareness and capacity-building programmes to tackle the causes of VAW, starting with training of doctors and health staff and later diversifying to community-level trainings.

After much discussion, the health department decided that the programme should kick off as a domestic violence management centre since that was the most common form of VAW. Locating the centre in a hospital would make it easier for women facing domestic violence to report there without fear of the perpetrator of violence finding out about their visit.

Prior to the launch of the programme, domestic violence was not considered a problem that needed to be addressed by health personnel. Injuries due to domestic violence were treated like any other injury unless specifically reported by the victim as a case of assault. In all such reported cases, the duty of the treating physician was to provide medical care and report the case to the police for legal action. Psychosocial care and counselling, safety and security, and shelter and rehabilitation of the victim were never considered priorities by the health staff. There was no active attempt to identify the hidden cases of domestic violence, nor were there any attempts to look for evidence of domestic violence even when it seemed obvious. Doctors were content with recording the statement of the survivor as it was, however improbable it sounded. In effect, women were prevented from disclosing a history of domestic violence through the combined effect of a non-conducive atmosphere, ignorance, and irresponsible provider attitudes coupled with the notion that domestic violence is a social issue and medical intervention is needed only to treat injuries and other health consequences.

The first phase

The health department launched the project jointly with the NRHM and with the support of the social justice department (SJD) and police. The gender-based violence management (GBVM) centres were named Bhoomika, meaning "platform," because they were envisaged as a platform to launch all health system activities for gender equity in the long term.

The centres were established via a circular issued by the director of health services, which detailed the process of establishment and the roles and responsibilities of each stakeholder. It explained that Bhoomika aimed to identify domestic and sexual violence survivors from the emergency, out-patient, and inpatient departments of hospitals. It also stressed the need to develop links with other departments and agencies to provide comprehensive care and support to survivors.

In 2009, the first phase of the programme was launched in 14 major hospitals (13 district hospitals and one taluka hospital) spread over the 14 districts of Kerala. The plan funds (Rs 50 lakh) earmarked by the KSPB were used for setting up the 14 centres, initial trainings, awareness-building, and publicity. The centres started functioning with one female counsellor, supported with NRHM funds, who was designated GBVM counsellor and coordinator. She had the dual responsibility of providing support and coun-selling to survivors of violence and coordinating awareness and training programmes in the hospital and other institutions in the district. In the first phase, the centres functioned from 9 am to 5 pm. Cases that came in outside work hours had to be admitted to the hospital or sent back with instructions to report the following day. In 2013, an additional counsellor was appointed with support from the SJD, and the centres' hours were extended from 7 am to 7 pm in two shifts. One of the counsellors was put on call (with vehicle facility) to attend to cases reported after working hours. In effect, the cen-tres began functioning 24 hours on working days, while cases reported on holidays remained unattended. With the Bhoomika initiative gaining popu-larity and demand from communities and local self-governments increasing, seven more centres were added in taluka hospitals – four in 2011–12, two in 2012–13, and one in 2013–14.

The duties of the GBVM counsellor were to:

1   Prepare a status report of the facilities available for survivors of domestic and sexual violence, first in the parent hospital and then at other hospitals in the district
2   Identify and register domestic violence cases reporting to the OPD, casualty, and inpatient departments of the hospital where the centre is functioning
3   Ensure quality care of GBV survivors (women and children), including medical care and psychological support
4   Provide assistance and support to survivors through links with the legal system, police, and shelter homes, where needed
5   Create networks with similar services already in place in the district, such as the Jagratha Samithis (vigilance committees) set up at the level of local government, for awareness-building and support for survivors at the grassroots
6   Build the capacity of stakeholders, especially doctors and paramedics, with the support of the master trainers in the district
7   Document the process of GBV interventions at the centres and in the district, including experiences gained from the project

Table 2.2.1 Organisational structure of Bhoomika

Institutional-level committee

1 Convener – senior female medical officer, preferably a gynaecologist or psychiatrist
2 Nursing superintendent
3 One casualty medical officer, preferably a woman
4 Psychiatrist/clinical psychologist
5 Surgeon
6 ENT surgeon
7 Orthopaedic surgeon
8 Paediatrician
9 Gynaecologist
10 Physician
11 One member from the hospital management committee, nominated by the chairman

District intersectoral committee

1 Superintendent of the hospital where the Bhoomika centre functions
2 Health standing committee chairman of district panchayat
3 District medical officer of health   .
4 District reproductive and child health (RCH) officer
5 District programme manager of NRHM
6 District superintendent of police
7 Female protection officer
8 Representatives from:
  i   Women's cell of police
  ii Social justice department
  iii Kerala State Legal Services Authority (KELSA)
  iv Leading NGOs
9 GBVM coordinator/counsellor

Source: Department of Health and Family Welfare, Government of Kerala.

The Bhoomika centres were managed at two levels: (i) at the institutional level by an institutional committee and (ii) at the district level by an inter-sectoral committee. The institutional committee Table 2.2.1) managed the day-to-day activities of the centre. The intersectoral committee at the district level advised and guided the activities of the centre and coordinated activities throughout the district.

Key roles of Bhoomika

The Bhoomika model focused principally on responding to survivors of domestic violence but also addressed sexual violence, exploitation, and abuse. The response included medical care of survivors, psychosocial care, and legal aid as well as provisions for the safety and security of the individual and a facility to act as a short-stay home where needed. It also aimed to generate awareness in the community about domestic violence, patriarchal

DEPARTMENT STATE NODAL OFFICE		
National Health Mission	Directorate of Health Services	Social Justice Department

DISTRICT NUCLEUS		District Intersectoral Committee
District RCH Officer	District Programme Manager (NHM)	• Health Department • Social Justice Department • Police • District Legal Services Society • Female Protection Officer • NGO Representatives

Institution	Institution-Level Committee
Superintendent of the Hospital	

Bhoomika
GBVM Counselor / Coordinator

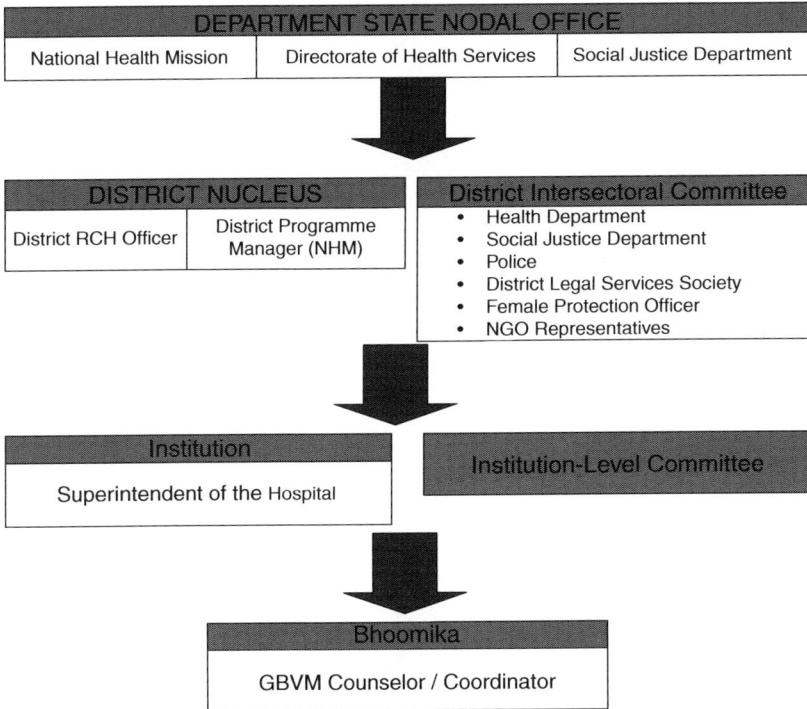

Figure 2.2.1 Organisational structure of Bhoomika centres
Source: Department of Health and Family Welfare, Government of Kerala.

social norms, and women's empowerment. The organisational structure of Bhoomika centres is depicted in Figure 2.2.1.

The Bhoomika centre was to act as the nucleus for the training of health professionals, including on-the-job and refresher trainings. Master trainers were appointed at the state level and a district training team was formed under the leadership of the district RCH officer (the nodal officer for coordinating the programme at the district level). The training team consisted of doctors, including gynaecologists and physicians, other paramedical professionals, legal experts, and police officials. This team trained all doctors and other health professionals in the district.

The district team also trained block-level teams, which then conducted awareness programmes at the grassroots through Kudumbasree units, ASHA volunteers, Jagratha Samithis, and local self-governments. Bhoomika also acted as a nodal centre for the training of allied departments concerned with service delivery to the survivor. It developed close links with other specialised service providers, referring survivors with special needs for psychotherapy, occupational rehabilitation, and economic support. Through trainings and regular review of the programme at the district-level conferences of medical officers and supervisors every month, a close link was maintained with the primary healthcare system in the district. This resulted in increased awareness among grassroots health workers and sustained motivation for them to inquire into incidents of domestic violence in their area and refer such cases to the Bhoomika centres. The district-level intersectoral committee and trainings at panchayat level ensured strong links with local self-governments.

The GBVM counsellor-coordinator was responsible for coordinating all the activities of the centre. She was assisted by the district- and block-level training teams in capacity-building and awareness generation. Support from the female protection officer appointed under the PWDVA and officials of the SJD, police, and Kerala State Legal Services Authority (KELSA) panel of advocates enabled her to provide various need-based services to survivors.

Engagement with the health system

Early experiences with the health system while setting up the Bhoomika centres were not very encouraging. The general attitude amongst doctors that anything they dealt with should be "treatable" presented the biggest problem in the management of GBV. Doctors regarded injury – whatever its cause – as a medical issue that needed treatment (suturing, dressings, drugs). How the injury occurred was not considered their mandate, except as required to rule out internal injuries. Who the perpetrator was, whether the woman was in a position to go back home safely, whether there was risk of further violence – all this was beyond their purview.

Given this mindset, Bhoomika presented a new challenge to them: here was an issue they could not cure with a pill. Other healthcare providers, including nursing staff, also initially considered Bhoomika outside their purview and hence an extra burden. This was why training for health professionals was essential. The training included basic concepts about gender and gender norms in society and how these are influenced by socialisation. Role-play activities based on real-life situations of dealing with survivors of GBV, especially survivors of rape, were eye-openers for the trainees. The trainings drove home the fact that GBV is not the fault of the survivor – as asserted by society – but the result of patriarchal social norms. With this training, attitudes slowly started changing, and over the years, doctors and staff have begun to support the programme.

Increasing awareness among health professionals, coupled with change in attitudes, has resulted in more survivors being identified and referred to the Bhoomika centres. While once medical attention would end with treatment of an injury, providers are now sensitive to the possibility of GBV and are suspecting it and enquiring about it. The casualty and outpatient departments referred the majority of cases, while trained nursing staff picked up some cases from the wards. Grassroots workers, police, and SJD officials referred a small percentage of women, while still fewer numbers walked in on their own. Sensitisation training given to doctors at primary health centres, junior public health nurses (JPHN), ASHAs, and Kudumbasree volunteers in the community resulted in identification and referral of more women from the community.

Engaging with the community

Initially, panchayat representatives and officials were apprehensive about the role Bhoomika would play, since according to them several mechanisms to tackle GBV were already in place, in the form of Jagratha Samithis, the police, and legal authorities. With repeated consultations, the Bhoomika team was able to drive home the point that the centres would stress medical care and psychosocial support to heal the psychological and emotional injury caused by violence rather than push for legal action against the perpetrator, which was the role of the police and legal system. The process would in fact support women identified by Jagratha Samithis and women who were not yet willing to go for legal action. The fact that Bhoomika could also provide counselling to the family to provide a better atmosphere for the woman to live in before going in for legal action gained acceptance in the community.

Achievements so far

Trainings

From inception in 2009 to March 2013, the Bhoomika team trained more than 21,000 persons from various categories (Table 2.2.2). Trainings have also been conducted for staff of the SJD (anganwadi workers and helpers), police, and education departments. Several people have attended awareness programmes at the grassroots level. It was realised that restricting trainings to the hospital set-up would deal with only the consequences of violence. To create awareness in the community, it was essential to deal with its causes. Therefore, the training and sensitisation programmes were targeted

Table 2.2.2 Details of various categories of health staff trained from 2009 to 2013

Doctors trained	2,036
Staff nurses trained	2,798
Field staff trained	7,464
ASHAs trained	9,273
Total	**21,571**

Source: Compiled by author.

to include key actors in the community, from ASHA and anganwadi workers to panchayati raj representatives, women's self-help groups (Kudumbasree), and other community and social leaders.

Case management

Table 2.2.3 provides details of the number of cases handled by the Bhoomika centres, Table 2.2.4 presents the classification of the types of cases, and Table 2.2.5 details further referrals from the Bhoomika centre.

Since the reporting system did not routinely collect details of the perpetrator or form of violence, an attempt was made to classify this based on a sample of cases from selected centres. The records of such cases were analysed, and Table 2.2.6 presents the findings.

Table 2.2.3 Number of cases dealt with by different Bhoomika centres year-wise (2009–14)

No.	Name of centre	2009– 10	2010– 11	2011– 12	2012– 13	2013– 14	April – December 2014	Total
1	Thiruvananthapuram	23	178	207	218	172	228	1,026
2	Neyyatinkara	0	0	0	0	0	132	132
3	Kollam	14	241	141	166	253	327	1,142
4	Karunagappally	0	0	21	0	4	156	181
5	Pathanamthitta	11	51	151	45	173	248	679
6	Alapuzha	16	157	160	0	167	297	797
7	Idukki	12	128	19	122	57	198	536
8	Thodupuzha	0	0	95	239	277	251	862
9	Kottayam	18	120	190	237	328	307	1,200
10	North Paravur	0	0	0	5	110	126	241
11	Ernakulam	20	234	216	280	262	203	1,215
12	Chavakkad	0	0	0	52	151	166	369
13	Thrissur	34	200	306	350	424	368	1,682
14	Alathur	0	0	98	138	241	261	738
15	Palakkad	24	257	278	243	312	264	1,378
16	Malappuram	15	105	180	198	220	139	857
17	Kozhikode	27	217	304	378	418	294	1,638
18	Vadakara	0	0	8	121	298	222	649
19	Wayanad	48	225	95	148	250	296	1,062
20	Kannur	18	137	175	237	243	197	1,007
21	Kasargod	26	152	168	215	275	235	1,071
	Total	306	2,402	2,812	3,392	4,635	4,915	18,462

Source: Compiled by author.

Table 2.2.4 Nature of cases dealt with by Bhoomika centres till March 2014*

No.	Nature of cases	Number
1	Domestic violence	7,843
2	Counselling and psychosocial care#	1,092
3	Suicide attempts	952
4	Rape and sexual abuse of various forms	347
5	Others	2,878

Source: Compiled by author.

* Many women who do not admit that they are suffering from domestic violence but still would like to use the counselling services provided by Bhoomika are seen at the centres. In addition, several adolescent children come for psychosocial support related to scholastic, emotional, and family issues

Table 2.2.5 Referral of cases by Bhoomika centres till March 2014

No.	Nature of cases	Number
1	Police	3,085
2	Legal services	1,299
3	Further medical care	672
4	Psychological/psychiatric support	1,231
5	Shelter homes/short-stay homes	128
6	Women protection officer	692
7	Others	940

Source: Compiled by author.

Table 2.2.6 Classification of chief perpetrator of violence in random selection of cases of domestic violence reported from January to March 2015 (%)

Intimate partner	49.3
Mother-in-law	11
Sister-in-law	6.2
Father-in-law	4.8
Son-in-law	0.7
Daughter-in-law	0.7
Husband's brother	3.8
Son	4.2
Father	2
Brother	2.4
Mother	0.9
Sister	2.9
Others	11

Source: Compiled by author.

Advantages of working with the health system

The Bhoomika programme was rooted in the health system from the out-set. The biggest advantage of this was the ease with which survivors could approach the centre for services. This was like approaching a hospital, as they had done previously, but with a transformed approach and atmosphere. Working through the health system gave the programme a big impetus because of the large number of grassroots-level workers reaching out to the community – a reach no other department could claim. The seriousness with which the community considered any advice or intervention from the health sector was an added advantage.

Concerns about working with the health system

In the initial phases of the programme, over-medicalisation was a matter of concern. The strong resistance of doctors to accepting GBV as a public health issue rather than a purely bio-medical issue was one of the initial constraints. But, beyond just domestic violence, the medical community considered any possibility of a medico-legal case problematic. The level of ignorance about relevant laws, including the PWDVA (2005), was unexpected. So it became imperative for Bhoomika to start working with the doctors and staff from scratch. It was through repeated trainings and regular interaction that a change in the attitude of the majority of doctors and other health personnel was accomplished. Health personnel gradually woke up to the fact that GBV was a health issue where the medical community had a major role to play – one that went far beyond its traditional curative role. A reformed medical community has sincerely taken up its responsibility to identify, manage, and support women with a history of domestic and sexual violence in the major-ity of centres.

Challenges

System-related challenges

The biggest challenge of working with the health system has been develop-ing community ownership of the programme. Five years after its launch, the programme had yet to find complete acceptance by the community. Though significant progress was made in sensitising different segments of the com-munity, including women's self-help groups, students, and various depart-ment officials, tackling the root causes of GBV at the community level was still a far-off dream.

The Bhoomika centres provide better care and support to women suffering various forms of domestic violence, but they are still not an integral part of the health system, and therefore reviews of psychosocial services have not become part of the programme. Follow-up of cases in the community and linkages with local mechanisms to provide home-based support are another big challenge. The reporting system did not collect data on referrals, and Bhoomika will have to address this to improve detection of cases in the community.

Employee-related challenges

When the centre was run with a single counsellor, she was overburdened with multiple responsibilities. There are two counsellors now, but the extension of service time to 24 hours has again increased their workload. The fact that counsellors have to coordinate the programme, liaise between different departments, and manage day-to-day issues also affects the quality of services provided. There is no on-job support to counsellors through skill upgradation or supportive supervision. High workload and lack of support systems are leading to burnout among the counsellors, adversely affecting their counselling skills. The absence of a proper documentation system has resulted in employee-related variations in the recording of case histories, which affects analysis as well as follow-up.

The way forward

With the Government of India announcing the Nirbhaya funds in 2013–14, various state governments were motivated to set up one-stop crisis centres (OSCCs) to help women and girls in distress due to gender-based violence. In 2014–15, Kerala also decided to implement the scheme. However, at a meeting of high-level officials of the health, social justice, and home departments, it was decided that since the health department already had the Bhoomika programme, a second set-up for the same purpose would be a duplication of efforts and a waste of resources. Instead, the government decided to make the Bhoomika centres a 24-hour service by appointing a second counsellor with the assistance of the SJD.

In the first five years of the programme, Bhoomika's on-site services were mainly medical and psychological support, with all other services, such as police aid and legal help, provided by the respective departments at their own premises. The Bhoomika centres are now in the process of upgradation to OSCCs where, along with the 24-hour service already begun, other services will be provided by respective departments at the Bhoomika centre itself. By end 2015, the 21 centres were in various stages of upgradation to OSCCs.

By 2015, even after five years of existence, no evaluation of the programme had been conducted. An analysis of Bhoomika's achievements and quality of services will bring out the gaps and constraints in the programme. Some reports are being compiled at the state level, but in the absence of further analysis, no action has been taken. An assessment of the performance followed by corrective action to improve quality of service is urgently needed.

The sheer number of cases being received at the Bhoomika centres drives home the fact that GBV is a grave public health issue in Kerala. Bhoomika should be strengthened further to enable it to venture into the preventive aspects of violence against women, which is the essence of public health. The caseload itself is an indication that the health system can no longer consider GBV a bio-medical issue, but one that requires concerted action at multiple levels – prevention of GBV, promotion of gender equity, and a multi-pronged approach to change social norms and attitudes.

References

INCLEN-ICRW (2000): *Domestic violence in India: Summary report of a multi-site household survey*, International Centre for Research on Women and International Clinical Epidemiologists Network, Washington, DC, United States of America.

Vijayan, A (2004): *A study on gender-based violence in Kerala*, Kerala: Sakhi Resource Centre for Women.

Vijayan, A and George, M S (2010): "Gender-responsive budgeting: The case of Kerala," Working Paper 3723, eSocialSciences.

2.3 Sukoon

Sonia Trikha Khullar and Manpreet Kaur

Sukoon centres, located at eight Civil Hospitals in Haryana, help survivors of VAW with medical treatment as well as psychological and legal counselling.

Introduction

Violence against women is a grave violation of human rights, with immediate and long-term physical, sexual, and psychological consequences for women and girls, including death. Wife-beating is considered justifiable to quite an extent in Haryana, where 32% of ever-married women have experienced spousal violence (NFHS-3[1]). Even during the sensitive phase of pregnancy, 5% of women in Haryana have experienced physical assault. Such pregnancies are high-risk because verbal, emotional, and physical abuse has negative health consequences – fatal and non-fatal – for the mother and foetus.

To address the medical, psychological, police-related, and legal needs of survivors of VAW, the State Health Systems Resource Centre (SHSRC) in Haryana set up a crisis intervention centre called Sukoon (meaning "relief" or "peace") at eight Civil Hospitals in the state. The Sukoon centres aim to address violence and foster women's empowerment and gender equality.

SHSRC, an autonomous body that advises the state government on planning and development of health and family welfare services, is the first government institution in Haryana to recognise the impact of violence on the health of women and child survivors.

Before initiating the process, SHSRC carried out a cross-sectional study of medico-legal records at Civil Hospital, Panchkula, Haryana. Analysis of the medico-legal cases from January to August 2013 revealed that a large number were related to violence against women. Of the 291 cases totally, 53% were physical assault cases, 1.4% were rape cases, and 15% were cases of poison consumption or other abuses.

A proposal was submitted to the additional chief secretary, health, Government of Haryana, for approval and funding of the centre. The state initially approved and funded one centre as a pilot project. Since the centre was located within the hospital, there was no requirement for a memorandum of understanding with the health department or hospital. From the next year

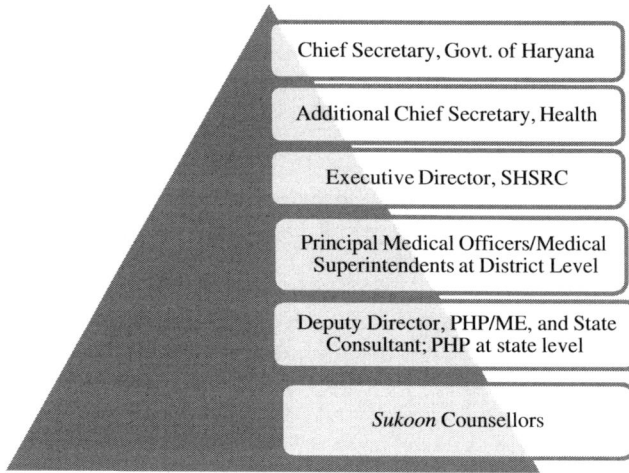

Figure 2.3.1 Organisational structure of Sukoon
Source: Compiled by authors.

onwards, the initiative and its budget were approved annually from the central government's NHM programme implementation plan (PIP).

The first Sukoon centre at Civil Hospital Panchkula was set up in 2014–15, followed by Civil Hospitals Ambala, Panipat, and Yamunanagar in the same year. Figure 2.3.1 presents the organisational structure of these centres. In 2017, more centres came up at the Civil Hospitals in Faridabad, Gurugram, Jind, and Rewari. The centres are located near gynaecology wards or trauma centres so that women survivors can access them easily. Sukoon counsellors, recruited by SHSRC, provide services at each centre and conduct active surveillance of violence cases among patients visiting the hospitals.

Key components of the model

Role of trained counsellors

- Helping survivors in getting investigations conducted and availing medical treatment at the Civil Hospitals
- Providing psychological counselling to address the emotional needs of survivors
- Assisting in registration of FIR in cases of sexual/physical assault and in further correspondence with the police department
- Helping survivors who want to file a case engage a lawyer who will work pro bono; a list of lawyers empanelled with the District Legal Services Authority is available at Sukoon centres

- Offering legal counselling on the rights of survivors and their families
- Conducting active surveillance in all departments of the Civil Hospital to identify probable survivors of violence who may otherwise go unattended due to the high patient load
- Sensitising healthcare providers on identification of abuse, provision of medical support to the survivor, examination, and documentation of cases of violence
- Sending child survivors to shelter homes such as Bal Niketan and Missionaries of Charity

Maintenance of database

The counsellors record the detailed history of each survivor in an intake sheet and enter it in Excel. Sukoon centres email the Excel sheets to the SHSRC office every fortnight/month. The counsellors maintain several registers, such as screening register, police record register, referral register, and follow-up register, for complete record-keeping.

Advocacy efforts

State-level convergence meeting

Addressing violence calls for a coordinated intersectoral response. Therefore, SHSRC brought various departments dealing with VAW together at a state-level convergence meeting in 2017–18, chaired by the chief secretary, Government of Haryana.

Sensitisation and capacity-building efforts

- *Training of Women Police Station (Mahila Thana) staff:* Two staffers from Mahila Thanas in each district of Haryana were trained on VAW at the State Institute of Health and Family Welfare (SIHFW), Panchkula, in 2017–18. They included women police officers of the rank of sub-inspector, assistant sub-inspector, and head constable. The additional director general of police, law, and order; inspector general of police, crimes against women; and principal secretary, health department, Government of Haryana, participated in the training.
- *Training of medical officers:* A five-day training on gender health mainstreaming was held for medical officers from 12 districts in 2017–18 at CEHAT, Mumbai.
- *Orientations for healthcare providers:* Medical officers and staff nurses have been oriented on the response to VAW on several occasions.
- *Induction and refresher trainings of Sukoon counsellors:* Several trainings have been conducted at SIHFW, Panchkula, and CEHAT, Mumbai.

- *Training of ASHA master trainers:* ASHAs are a key communication link between the healthcare system and rural populations. Their role in addressing violence through engagements with the community is crucial. ASHA master trainers (two from each district) were provided two-day trainings by resource persons from the State Health Resource Centre, Chhattisgarh, in September 2018. The training aimed to orient ASHAs on identifying survivors and responding to violence against women through interactive sessions, role-play, and group activities.
- *Trainings at educational institutions:* Sukoon counsellors regularly conduct meetings and trainings at schools and colleges. Patients and their attendants are also oriented about Sukoon centres at the obstetrics and gynaecology department, emergency, and OPDs.
- *Review meetings:* Periodic review meetings with counsellors at SHSRC assess the progress and functioning of Sukoon centres, update the counsellors about various legislations and guidelines, and address operational and implementation issues.

Technical and operational resource material

SHSRC has developed a Counsellor's Handbook on responding to violence against women and children to add value to the work of counsellors. A similar guidebook has been prepared for health professionals. Leaflets on VAW and the Sukoon centres have been distributed to general audiences.

Posters, flex boards, wall paintings, and signage at OPDs, registration counters, patient waiting areas, and gynaecology and emergency departments increase the visibility of the Sukoon centres.

Achievements and challenges

With the sensitisation of people on VAW, growing awareness about the Sukoon centres, and proactive measures by the counsellors, the number of survivors approaching Sukoon has increased (Figure 2.3.2).

There are plans to expand the Sukoon centres to more districts in 2018–19.

More than 3,700 survivors of GBV have received assistance of various kinds from inception of the Sukoon centres in 2014 to December 31, 2018. As seen in Figure 2.3.3, physical assault accounts for 65% of the cases and sexual assault (including rape) for 25%. Ten percent of the cases classified as other forms of violence included suicide attempts, poisoning, and burns.

Although the cost-effectiveness of the Sukoon centres has not been quantified, the budget required to set up and maintain these centres is modest, as only two counsellors are required.

The main challenge faced by all Sukoon counsellors is the absence of a sufficient number of shelter homes for women surviving violence. In many cases, the survivor cannot go back home since the perpetrator is present. Her

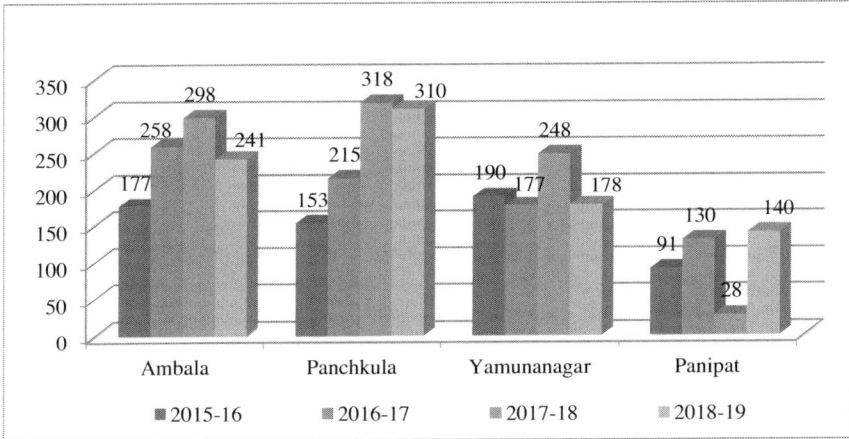

Figure 2.3.2 District-wise distribution of cases until December 31, 2018 (n = 3,152)
Source: Compiled by authors.

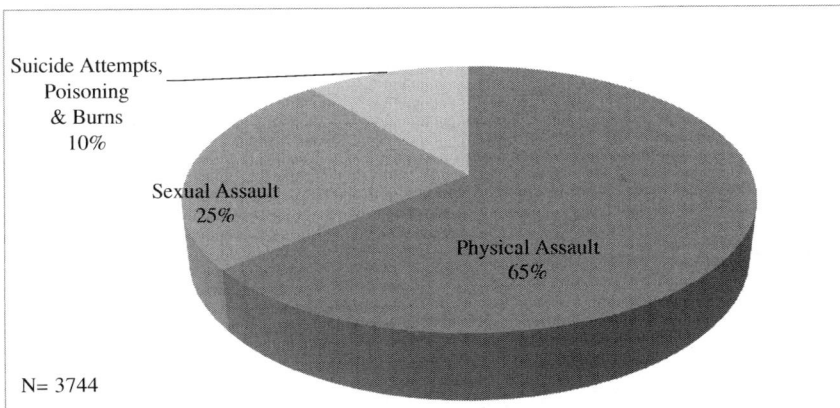

Figure 2.3.3 Sukoon cases according to type of violence
Source: Compiled by authors.

parents may not be in a position to have her back. Due to high patient load, the survivor can be hospitalised for only a short period.

Lessons and recommendations

Establishing tie-ups with the local police department, lawyers, and shelter homes is vital for provision of services. Sustained sensitisation of the healthcare staff is also crucial for acceptance of the programme at the health facility level.

Counsellors need to undergo regular trainings to improve their skills. Documentation and record-keeping are essential to the functioning of a crisis intervention centre.

Note

1 International Institute for Population Sciences (IIPS) and ICF (2017): *National Family Health Survey (NFHS-3), 2005–2006: India*, Mumbai: IIPS.

2.4 Upscaling of Dilaasa

Sangeeta Rege, Padma Bhate-Deosthali, and Chitra Joshi

The upscaling of CEHAT's Dilaasa hospital-based crisis centre model to 11 hospitals in Mumbai indicates a systems approach to VAW, with complete ownership of the programme by the hospital.

Introduction

The Centre for Enquiry into Health and Allied Themes (CEHAT) has been working on the right to healthcare for all as well as the prevention of violence and provision of care for survivors. Since 1991, the organisation has investigated human rights violations through fact-finding missions and studies. CEHAT has also been developing training resources and conducting trainings.

In 1998, CEHAT organised an international conference on preventing violence and caring for survivors. The conference brought together evidence of violence against women and children, caste and communal violence, state participation in violence through torture of people in custody, state institutions perpetrating violence, and the role of medical/health professionals. CEHAT's own research evidence, along with country evidence, paved the way for a health sector response to violence against women. There was adequate evidence indicating that survivors of VAW reach health providers seeking treatment of the health consequences of violence. The health sector is a crucial point of contact that allows health providers to respond to violence and mitigate its consequences. Responding to domestic violence was the starting point for engaging with the public health system to recognise its role in responding to domestic violence.

In the same year, CEHAT undertook a community action research project – a project situated in an urban slum community – titled Arogyachya Margavar, which aimed to study the determinants and levels of violence against women, identify the perpetrators of violence, and examine the help-seeking behaviour and coping strategies of women facing violence. The project trained community health workers to respond to domestic violence as well as the reproductive health needs of women. Simultaneously, CEHAT was engaged in discussions and dialogue with senior administrators of the Municipal Corporation of Greater Mumbai (MCGM) to initiate the setting up of a public hospital-based crisis centre to respond to violence against women.

The women's movement in India since the early 1980s brought the issue of violence against women to public attention. It examined different institutions, such as law enforcement agencies, and demanded services for women experiencing violence. The movement was instrumental in bringing about changes in the law and convincing the government to set up shelters for women and improve redressal mechanisms in the police station. However, there was little engagement with the health system other than the critique that health service providers were insensitive to the needs of those facing violence.

Dilaasa, a hospital-based crisis centre, was the first attempt in India to engage the public health system to recognise and respond effectively to violence against women and children. It was envisaged as a joint initiative of MCGM and CEHAT and was set up in 2000 at the K B Bhabha Hospital in Mumbai. Having generated evidence of the feasibility and effectiveness of setting up a hospital-based centre, CEHAT advocated for its uptake in several states. To recognise psychosocial services as an important component of health services, the model, accompanied by a clear budget, had to find its place within policy discourse. CEHAT continued to generate evidence of the cost of setting up such centres, its reach to women and girls in reproductive ages, scope for early identification of violence, and nature of health effects due to violence.

Keshav Desi Raju, principal secretary, MoHFW, examined the evidence and directed the Maharashtra health department and MCGM to integrate Dilaasa centres in the National Urban Health Mission (NUHM) 2014. Dilaasa was included in the National Urban Health Mission's Programme Implementation Plan (NUHM, PIP) for 2015–16, and 11 new Dilaasa centres were set up in MCGM hospitals.

This case study presents the setting up of the 11 new Dilaasa centres and the insights gained from this replication.

Objectives and approach to the replication of Dilaasa

The Dilaasa departments were set up with the primary objective of providing psychosocial services to women and children facing violence. The second objective was to enable hospitals to recognise violence as a health issue and institutionalise a healthcare response to survivors.

The important components of Dilaasa included:

1   Sensitising health professionals to violence against women, building their capacities to conduct similar sensitisation programmes for their peers, and legitimising violence against women as a crucial public health concern
2   Setting up psychosocial services for women and children facing violence as part of hospital services

As Dilaasa was conceptualised as a hospital department, it was to be headed by the medical superintendent of the hospital. The Dilaasa departments would provide crisis intervention services to women and children facing violence and train healthcare providers to recognise signs of violence and provide care and refer them to Dilaasa. In addition, Dilaasa worked to bring on board a set of middle- to senior-level health providers and build their capacities to orient hospital staff to the issue of VAW. This served two purposes: firstly, training by their peers lent legitimacy to the issue of VAW and communicated the message that responding to VAW was the responsibility of the hospital and, secondly, it increased ownership of the Dilaasa centre amongst hospital staff. The core group played an important role in integrating the services of the centre in hospital services. One of the doctors of the core group was appointed the nodal officer for Dilaasa and was consulted by the Dilaasa team whenever they encountered challenges with the police or hospital staff.

The staff and infrastructure mandated under the NUHM were based on the 2000 Dilaasa model.

Staff at Dilaasa

- Nodal officer
- Two counsellors with a postgraduate degree in the social sciences, such as social work or psychology
- Two auxiliary nurse midwives
- A data entry operator to manage the management information system (MIS) at the centre

Designated space

- Each hospital would provide a separate space within the main outpatient department.
- The Dilaasa centre would be provided an intercom number that assists coordination with other hospital departments for services required.

Infrastructure

- Each Dilaasa centre would be provided a cupboard, desks, chairs, and curtains under the NUHM grant.
- Petty cash would be available for expenses related to women, such as food, travel to the home, and so on.
- Registers and intake forms would be provided to the centres under the grant.

Key activities of Dilaasa centres

Provision of crisis intervention services

Dilaasa counsellors appointed by NUHM came from different backgrounds, such as social work, women's studies, and psychology. As technical partner to MCGM, CEHAT conducted a five-day training course to familiarise counsellors with feminist perspectives on violence against women and children and give them an understanding of the health consequences of VAW and the skills to implement crisis intervention services. These counsellors have made several efforts to establish themselves in the hospital system. They have developed skills to decipher medical records of patients in the OPD and in the wards to understand their health conditions and their association with VAW. Counsellors visit the emergency ward every morning to scan the medico-legal register and check whether any cases related to VAW have been admitted in the hospital. As part of crisis counselling, they discuss the impact of violence on women's health, assess the intensity of violence, and develop safety plans along with women. Women are encouraged to record police complaints to create evidence of the violence faced. If women are scared or reluctant to do so, counsellors initiate contact with the police and assist them in recording police complaints. Given the workload at the hospital, it is not feasible for them to accompany every woman to the police station; therefore, many counsellors have established a rapport with police stations so that the police respond to their calls.

ANMs designated at each of the Dilaasa centres are equipped to carry out health talks in OPDs with patients and distribute information, education, and communication (IEC) material related to violence and health. They also visit different wards and speak to nurses and support staff to look for signs and symptoms of violence in patients admitted. Besides this, ANMs are involved in outreach work, visiting communities and talking about Dilaasa services. This has resulted in increased awareness about the Dilaasa centres in hospitals.

Strong linkages with legal aid services

The Dilaasa centres also connect with protection officers under the PWDVA and free legal aid lawyers. The counsellors realised early on that women do not easily get assistance from the lawyers and protection officers, either because they are overworked or because they demand money from the women. Counsellors took such lawyers to task by making formal complaints to the higher authorities and ensured that women did not have to bribe them to do their jobs. The counsellors contact the lawyers every month to follow up on the legal status of cases filed.

Creating a network for social support

Every Dilaasa centre has established contact with organisations, income-generation programmes and skill-building programmes, with the understanding that women and girls who deal with violence may also need work and the skills to make them employable and independent. Dilaasa has enabled a choice of different occupations, such as taxi driver, home guard services, and mall work.

Box 2.4.1 provides an example of actively identifying survivors of violence against women and children.

Box 2.4.1   Identifying cases of VAW at hospitals

A Dilaasa ANM came across a 13-year-old girl accompanying her ill aunt to the hospital. As she distributed pamphlets to patients, she found the girl reading one and therefore started talking to her. The child revealed that her mother was engaged in sex work and one of the customers would sexually abuse her. Though she had raised the issue with her mother, she took no action. The girl told the ANM that she did not want to live with her mother and wanted to find another place to stay and study. The ANM contacted the Dilaasa counsellor, and they explored the possible options, including any family member who could take the child in.

In the course of the discussions, the child also revealed that she feared for the safety of her younger sister. When the counsellors had gained the child's trust, she said she feared being sold into the sex trade. This was clearly a crisis situation, as the child could not go back to the same surroundings.

After explaining and preparing the girl for the child welfare committee (CWC) procedure and shelter home, the police were contacted and an FIR was filed. During her second hearing at the CWC, the CWC members asked the child if she wished to go back to her home, but she clarified that she wanted to stay at the shelter and continue her studies.

This story illustrates the team effort from counsellors and healthcare providers as they engage with multiple agencies to resolve each case – contacting the police, recording a complaint, locating an appropriate shelter, preparing the child to stay at the shelter, and presenting the facts to the CWC.

Ongoing training of healthcare providers

Two mid-level doctors and two senior nurses from each hospital were deputed for a nine-day training course on violence against women and the role of healthcare providers. These nine days were spread over four months (roughly two days every month), as it is not possible for hospitals to spare personnel for several days at a stretch. The training course provided an in-depth knowledge of gender and sex, discrimination, forms of violence against women, intersectionality as a concept, national and international evidence of the consequences of violence, the role of healthcare providers in responding to violence, including medico-legal aspects, and first-line care to be offered to survivors. The last part of the training equipped participants to design a two-hour orientation for their peers once they went back to their respective hospitals.

Setting up these core groups was an important element in the Dilaasa programme, as the health providers at the hospital needed to own the crisis centres; the counsellors and healthcare providers were required to be one unit at the level of Dilaasa. After these trainings, short orientations were initiated at each of the hospitals. In the beginning, the CEHAT team handheld the core group members in conducting these sessions.

Figure 2.4.1 provides a snapshot of the protocols followed by Dilaasa centres and highlights of the model.

These trainings are ongoing and are conducted for existing staff as well as newly recruited resident medical officers. The Dilaasa module has now been integrated into the "hospital orientation" programme as well. These programmes are held every six months for a batch of new resident medical officers, orienting them to the different departments and hospital systems. The integration of Dilaasa services into this package is an important step towards recognising it as one more department of the hospital. Besides these initiatives at the hospital, the Dilaasa department also takes orientation trainings of community health workers (CHWs) who have close contact with women and children in the community. ANMs also make CHWs aware of the signs and symptoms of violence against women and its effect on health and provide information on the different crisis centres across hospitals in Mumbai.

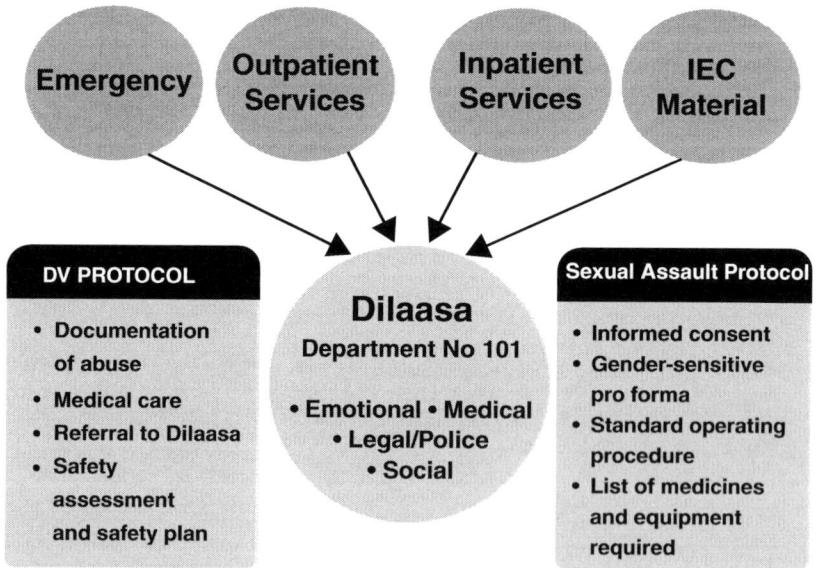

Figure 2.4.1 Dilaasa crisis centres

Source: Compiled by authors.

Consistent trainings, orientations, and poster/pamphlet distribution by Dilaasa ANMs have enabled healthcare providers to identify the consequences of violence and refer women and children to Dilaasa.

Figures 2.4.2 and 2.4.3 provide information on the number of domestic violence survivors recorded at the Dilaasa crisis centres and their follow up; while Figures 2.4.5 and 2.4.5 provide the number of rape survivors responded to and followed up. The data are of women who were availed of Dilaasa services between April 2016 and June 2018.

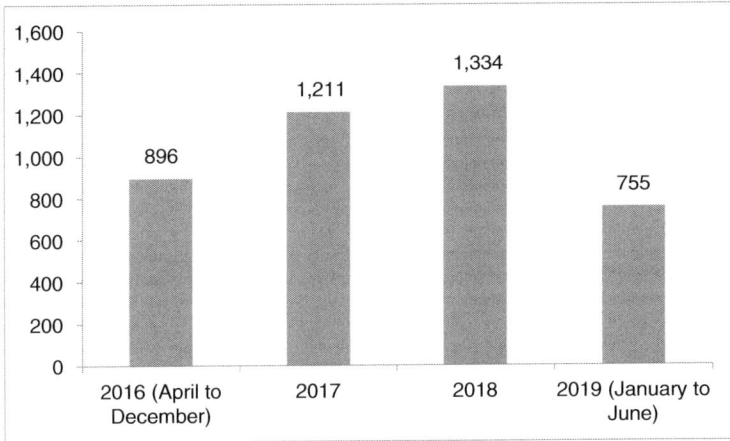

Figure 2.4.2 Number of cases of domestic violence (April 2016 to June 2019)
Source: Compiled by authors.

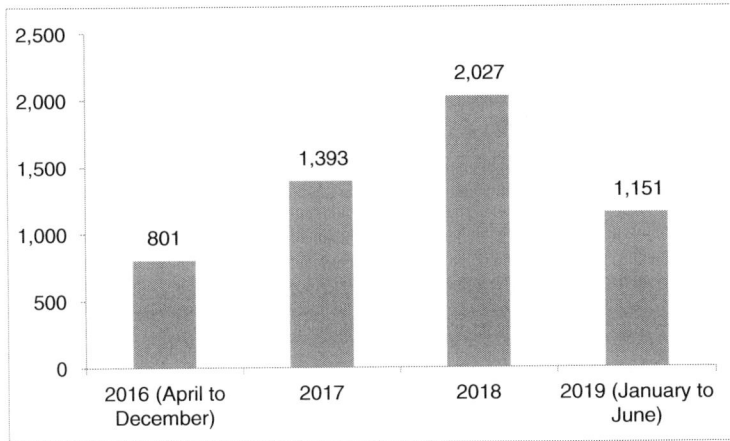

Figure 2.4.3 Number of domestic violence cases followed up (April 2016 to June 2019)
Source: Compiled by authors.

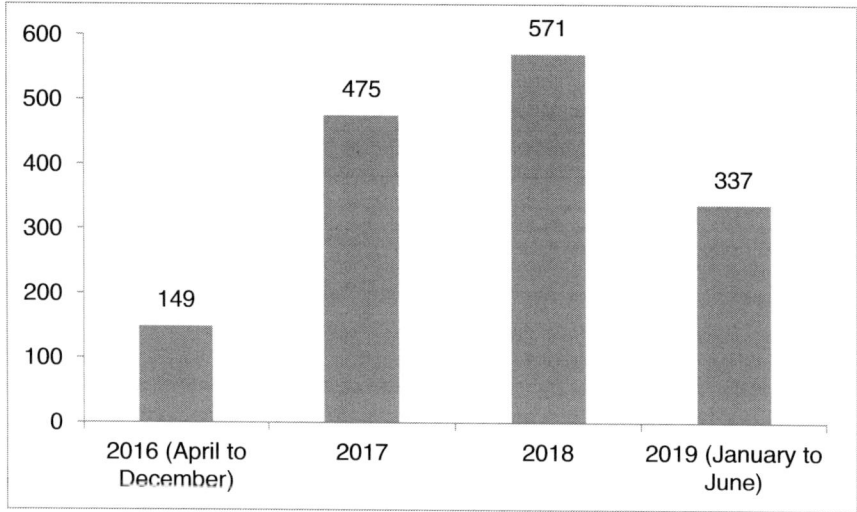

Figure 2.4.4 Number of cases of sexual violence (April 2016 to June 2019)
Source: Compiled by authors.

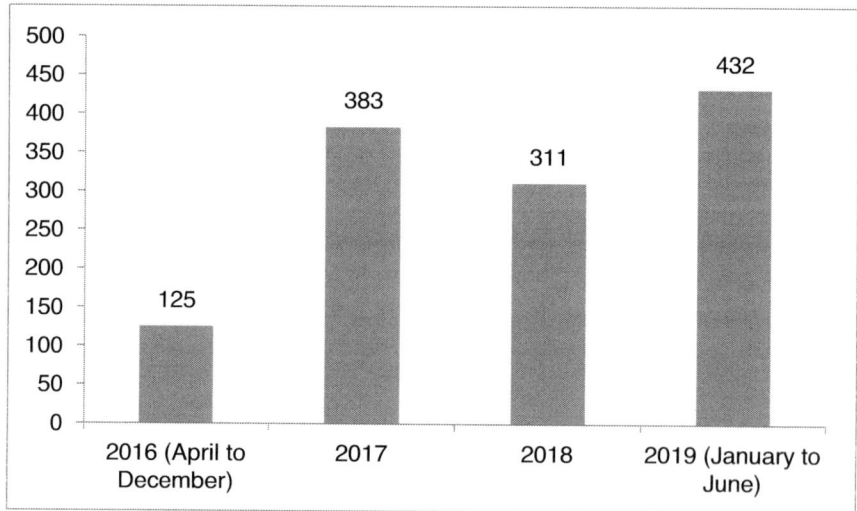

Figure 2.4.5 Number of sexual violence cases followed up (April 2016 to June 2019)
Source: Compiled by authors.

Achievements of Dilaasa

The replication of Dilaasa at 11 centres indicates a systems approach to violence against women. Dilaasa is a two-pronged programme: at one level, it is a counselling department offering services to women and children facing violence; at another, it enables the entire hospital system to recognise violence as a health issue and play a role in responding to survivors. This response goes beyond a clinical enquiry by doctors and nurses into symptoms associated with VAW. Health providers play an equivalent role in training new recruits, developing standard procedures for cogent response, and integrating Dilaasa as a department of the hospital. The core groups formed in each hospital have established that key healthcare providers are responsible for introducing new staff to standard operating procedures (SOPs) for domestic and sexual violence survivors, carrying out orientation trainings and playing a role in monitoring the quality of care received by survivors. The protocols detail all the steps to be taken at the hospital level from the time a survivor enters the hospital until she exits it. The SOPs lay down clear roles for doctors and nurses once they identify a survivor. Care is taken to ensure confidentiality as well as privacy of the woman/child. The hospital documentation system (case papers and registers) integrates a referral to Dilaasa, in effect formalising the referral system. Systematic record-keeping at Dilaasa through the intake forms helps generate evidence of the nature and extent of violence, its health impact, and women's expectations from the centre. These are critical in developing appropriate responses at different levels of the health system and can assist in designing health programmes inclusive of a response to VAW.

In the three years the Dilaasa centres have been operational, more than 3,000 survivors have been responded to across 11 hospitals. Figure 2.4.6 provides information on the number of women and children responded to by the Dilaasa crisis centres, while Figure 2.4.7 provides a breakdown of age ranges to which these survivors belonged.

Fifteen hundred healthcare providers, ranging from doctors and nurses to support staff, have been oriented to Dilaasa functions and given the skills to identify and respond to survivors sensitively. Figure 2.4.8 provides information on the pathways by which women and children seek Dilaasa services. A large number of referrals take place from the hospital, indicating consistent training and dialogue with health care providers to respond to VAW. The number of women using the Dilaasa services clearly indicates that hospitals are safe spaces for women to seek support and that they will not be questioned at home when they come to the Dilaasa centre on the pretext of a hospital visit. Similarly, serious cases with health consequences, such as violence in pregnancy, attempted suicide, and assaults, receive immediate service, including police and legal aid, while in the past they would have received medical care only. Figures 2.4.9 and 2.4.10 depict the types of violence suffered by survivors and its physical and psychological health consequences.

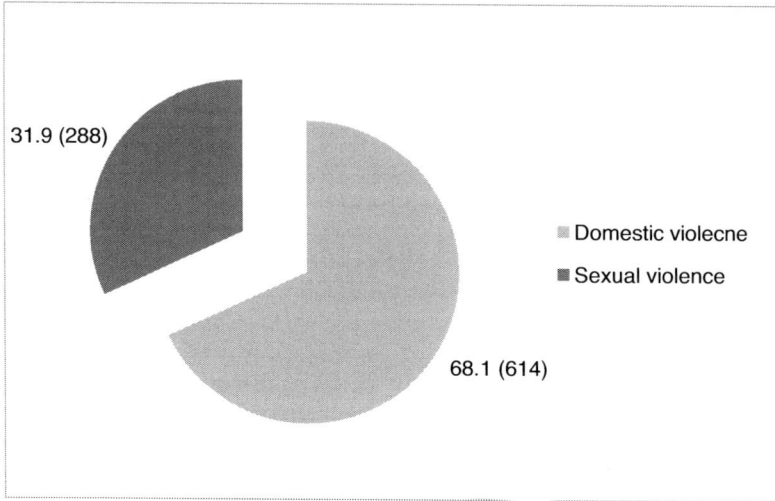

Figure 2.4.6 Types of cases (August 2018 to January 2019) (%) (total number of cases = 902)

Source: Compiled by authors.

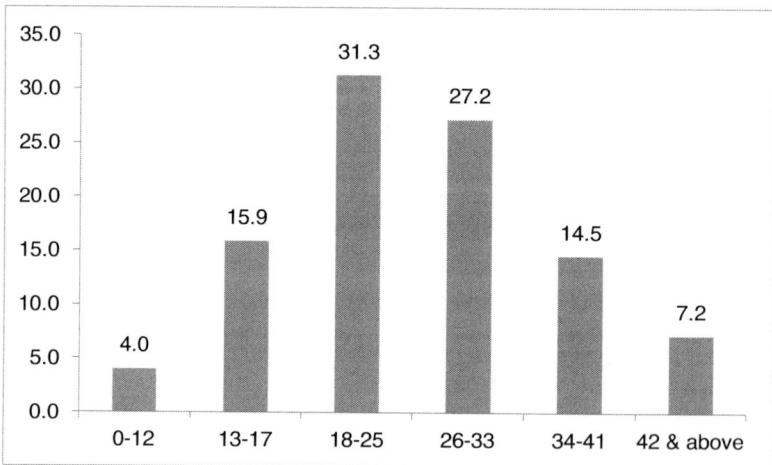

Figure 2.4.7 Age group of women registered at Dilaasa centres (August 2018 to January 2019)

Source: Compiled by authors.

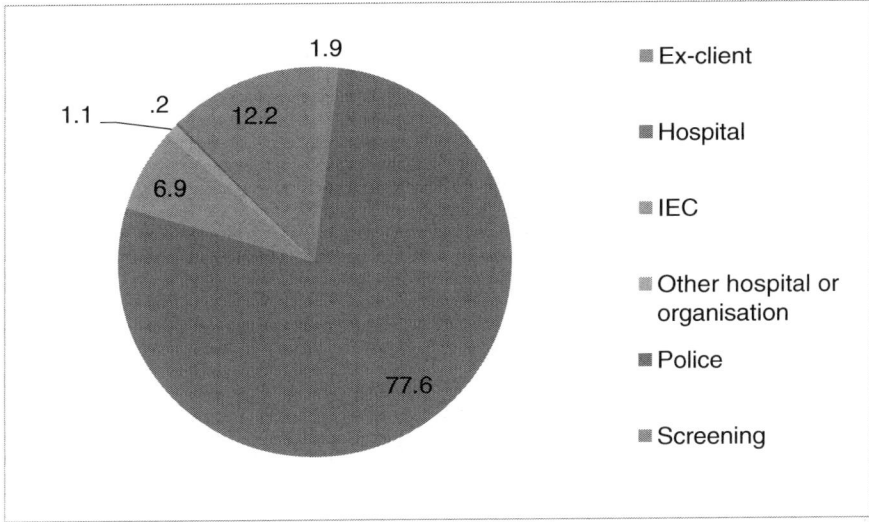

Figure 2.4.8 Pathway to Dilaasa centres (%) (August 2018 to January 2019)
Source: Compiled by authors.

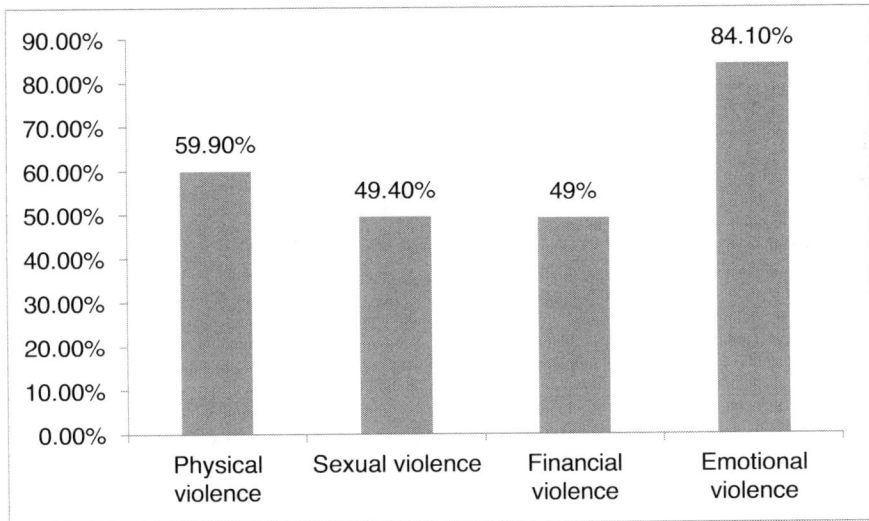

Figure 2.4.9 Types of violence (August 2018 to January 2019)
Source: Compiled by authors.

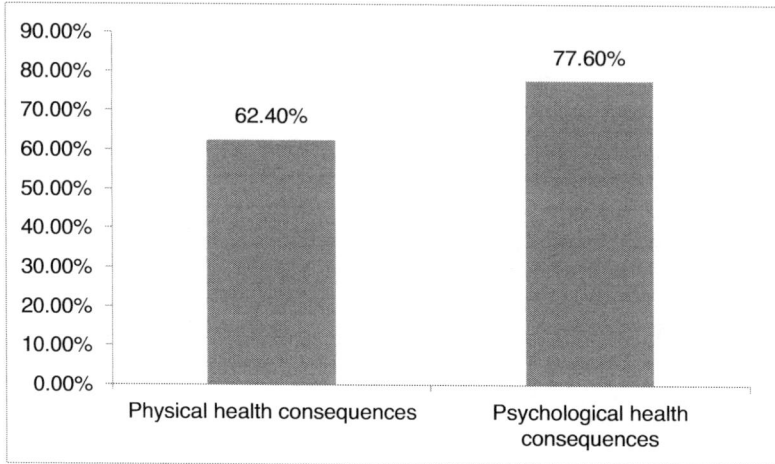

Figure 2.4.10 Health consequences reported by women (August 2018 to January 2019)

Source: Compiled by authors.

Lessons learnt

The Dilaasa centres have replicated the mandated MIS, but the hospitals also need to develop a mechanism for surveillance of the nature of cases being identified and referred from each hospital department. Not all women will seek Dilaasa services immediately, so maintaining a database would enable an understanding of the nature of health consequences and facility-level prevalence of VAW/G.

It is well established that counsellors need a forum to present their challenges and dilemmas, develop new skills, and continue to engage meaningfully in the prevention and response to VAW. At present CEHAT, as the technical partner to MCGM, facilitates such a forum, but this process needs to be institutionalised by the hospitals.

Although the Dilaasa team is designated to only respond to violence against women, hospital administrations often pull in Dilaasa staff for registration of patients, indenting work and so on. Dilaasa staff is recruited under the NUHM budget by the public health department and therefore is not seen as "core hospital staff." It is important to ensure that the Dilaasa team reports either to the medical superintendent or to the nodal officer designated by the medical superintendent.

The centres do not have a designated phone number, so counsellors and ANMs end up using their personal resources to follow up with survivors and others. Getting through to the hospital board line and contacting Dilaasa is also a cumbersome procedure for women.

Section 3

Working with hospitals

Introduction: establishing services for violence against women at public hospitals

This section presents the efforts of five organisations to set up psychosocial services within the health sector for women and children facing violence. Three of the organisations are feminist groups and two are health research and action groups. These CSOs have collaborated with the health system at the local and state levels to underline the need for a health system response to survivors of violence. They provide services within the health sector but with limited support from the healthcare system. Of the five, Soukhya collaborates with primary health centres and SWATI provides its services at a rural hospital, while Vimochana, SNEHA, and Anweshi work at tertiary hospitals in cities.

Vimochana has been creating awareness of violence against women since the 1970s, and Anweshi and SWATI since early 1990s. All three organisations have a feminist perspective and decades of experience in working with survivors of VAW. Their rationale for engaging with the health system was that women should receive sensitive and comprehensive services within hospitals, and now they are also filling the gap in psychosocial support services at health facilities for survivors of VAW.

Vimochana was one of the earliest feminist organisations in India. It was set up in the late 1970s and has worked on a range of issues, from the rights of women workers in the unorganised sector to rape, dowry deaths, and domestic violence. Its focus has been on public campaigns to increase awareness in the community, and it has demanded accountability from the police, lawmakers, and community. Early in the course of its work, Vimochana stumbled upon cases of women dying of burn injuries in the burn ward of a tertiary hospital. It observed the serious lacunae in the hospital response and set up a desk at the ward to provide services to patients and work with the broader medical system to improve the quality of burn care. Vimochana's review of the cause of these burns – the so-called "kitchen deaths" – revealed that these deaths were not accidental at all; they were associated with domestic violence. Its campaigns called out the gaps in the police investigation of these kitchen deaths as well as the inadequate response of the health sector when such women were admitted for burns. The Vimochana case study traces its interventions in the health system, which began with public protests and demands for accountability, better care for survivors of violence, and medico-legal documentation of cases and extended to providing care and support for survivors/victims of burns caused by domestic violence.

By the late 1980s, there was increased awareness of dowry deaths and bride burnings in India thanks to the campaigns conducted by the women's movement. The activists who set up Anweshi were inspired by Bodhana, an organisation that set up action committees at the community level to raise awareness of domestic violence and to take action against abusive families. They felt the need for direct services for women survivors, services that did not exist in the early 1990s. Thus, Anweshi was set up to provide counselling services for women facing violence. Its feminist counselling services were later expanded to legal services and shelter homes as well. The idea of engaging directly with the health sector on violence against women was born after Anweshi's interaction with the Dilaasa hospital-based crisis centre in Mumbai. The Anweshi case study provides insights on the role of training and advocacy in integrating the issue of VAW in mainstream health services. It also outlines its relationship with a public hospital and the creation of a network for referral of women and children to Anweshi for services. Although the hospital it collaborates with has not yet integrated counselling into its mainstream services, Anweshi has been able to create awareness not just amongst patients and relatives but also amongst health providers in hospital departments. It fills a crucial gap in "feminist counselling services" for women facing violence. Feminist counselling aims to reassure the affected woman that violence is not "normal," that it is not her fault, that it is unacceptable, and that something can be done to stop the abuse.

SWATI's interface with the health system began with trainings on the importance of medico-legal evidence for members of the Mahila Nyaya Panchayats (MNPs), which it had set up in the villages where it operated. MNP members were trained to accompany women facing domestic violence to police stations, and SWATI saw how difficult it was for them to access medico-legal records. This prompted SWATI to initiate a dialogue with hospital systems on the role it could play in responding to survivors of VAW. If health providers were trained to identify the signs and symptoms of VAW, SWATI recognised, they could set up counselling services at the hospital and establish links with the MNPs once a woman left the hospital. This would enable survivors to get a continuum of care within the community. The SWATI case study presents the experiences of rural counsellors who have been equipped to provide services at the level of the hospital and to engage with the health system for a clear referral system. SWATI also got villagers to question the abusive behaviour of men and understand the need to support women through the legal process.

SNEHA and Soukhya's initiatives are slightly different: their engagements with the health system had the specific goal of sensitising the health sector on the need to respond to VAW and equipping healthcare providers to respond to VAW, ensuring service provision for survivors in the process.

SNEHA's approach to VAW has always been viewed through the health-care lens. Set up in 1999, SNEHA focused on improving the health of women by mitigating domestic violence. To understand the underlying reasons for poor nutrition and poor health, the founders of SNEHA visited urban communities around the hospital where they worked. They found that several social issues affect health-seeking behaviour and health outcomes, but that violence against women is a very significant factor hindering good health. The SNEHA case study describes the strategies adopted to enable community women and adolescents to prevent violence against women and, where such violence has already occurred, to provide crisis intervention services. Thus, SNEHA's response to VAW began at the community level and moved gradually to public hospitals and the setting up of "women's OPDs" to respond to violence against women. Their case study outlines the importance of linkages between the community and the formal health system in responding to VAW.

Soukhya, a joint project of St John's Medical College and the Bengaluru Municipal Corporation, had a similar genesis. Researchers from St John's Medical College hypothesised that increasing awareness of VAW and its health consequences amongst communities would enable women to make the connection between violence and health and seek out health services. The project was based on earlier research conducted by St John's Medical Institute on the association between VAW and health. Based on the findings, the project aimed (i) to create awareness about violence against women and health among front-line workers, (ii) to carry out a sensitive enquiry by doctors and nurses on VAW, and (iii) to develop a referral mechanism whereby counsellors could meet these women at a health centre convenient to them. A unique feature of the project was the setting up of a system of mobile counsellors who were available across different health centres run by the municipal corporation. The Soukhya case study underlines the critical role that different levels of the health system can play in responding to violence against women.

Common to all five case studies is the building of an effective partnership with the health system without losing the core values of social change to end violence against women. Each case study has a set of strategies unique to its setting: ensuring the early involvement of health administrators, generating evidence to communicate the extent of the health effects of violence, and, most importantly, filling the gap by providing crisis counselling services to women and children.

All these initiatives aimed to sensitise health workers and health facilities to domestic violence and provide services to women coming to these facilities, but they did not aim to institutionalise services within the system. In fact, the health facilities seemed happy to have the CSOs provide the services.

The large number of women supported by these initiatives is indicative of the need for a health system response to VAW. SNEHA has carried out systematic research to highlight the number of women coming to health facilities for treatment of the health consequences of violence. All five organisations have faced a lot of resistance from health staff but have continued their dialogue and been allowed a presence at the facilities.

SNEHA and SWATI focus on service provision for women coming to health facilities, but they also have a backward link to other programmes at the community level. Both have been able to show the upward referral from community health workers to rural hospitals and tertiary care hospitals. Vimochana has retained its focus on burn care and has confined its work to the burn ward of a tertiary hospital.

3.1 Vimochana

Donna Fernandes, K Satyadevi, and Padma Bhate-Deosthali

Vimochana's intervention at Victoria Hospital in Bengaluru has set new standards for the health system's response to burn care for victims of domestic violence.

Introduction

Vimochana evolved from the CIED Collective formed in the 1970s to provide a platform for those in search of political transformation. Formally established in 1979, after the Emergency, by women from diverse social and economic backgrounds, Vimochana was ideologically located at the intersections of feminism, socialism, and non-violent forms of action. Vimochana identifies, examines, and attempts to resolve issues related to women's oppression in India and focuses on the development of women's consciousness. It has run campaigns on the rights of women workers in the unorganised sector as well as rape, domestic violence, dowry, and unnatural deaths of women. The group has also provided support to individual women, carrying out necessary investigations and documentation. As Vimochana grew, it began to attract membership from both victims of violence themselves and their families.

In 1995, the death of a woman due to a "stove burst" caught Vimochana's attention. Its initial concern was ensuring the ban of such dangerous stoves. However, the ambiguous manner in which incidents of stove bursts were reported raised the suspicions of Vimochana volunteers. The stove bursts were being attributed to accidents, such as falling kitchen objects and utensils, which seemed unlikely to inflict such serious – often fatal – burn injuries. Additionally, the victims seemed to be reporting in a manner that suggested they were being pressured to furnish inaccurate details. The frequency of these reports was cause for concern. Even more disconcerting was the fact that the police neglected to follow up these cases and were ready to dismiss them at face value. The lack of strong evidence of how the stoves burst, coupled with the unconvincing investigations by the police, led the volunteers to investigate further themselves. They uncovered some shocking facts.

As a spin-off of the stove burst incidents, in 1997, Vimochana launched a campaign on women's right to live. They studied the cases recorded as "unnatural deaths" and found that they included several covered up murders, suicides, and so-called "kitchen accidents." Vimochana went to the residences of women who had died and spoke to their neighbours and families. The investigations revealed that these women had, in fact, died of harassment and not stove bursts. The volunteers were able to establish this only because they acted diligently on initial suspicion. They found several procedural lapses, such as cases being registered only after the death of the victim, and post-mortems, dying declarations, and inquests not being conducted properly. Another alarming discovery was that none of the stoves in the so-called "stove burst" cases were seized! The doctors and police appeared to believe – without probing – the feeble reasons given by the victims or their in-laws as the cause of the accident, including bizarre claims of rodents knocking down stoves. This pointed to the police's lack of commitment to the investigation and collection of evidence.

One such woman who suffered 54% burns and reported stove burst as the cause was Mangal. However, on enquiry with neighbours, it emerged that she was a case of attempted homicide. The Vimochana team found evidence in the house that proved the incident had occurred not in the kitchen but on another floor. The patient finally revealed that she did not want the family to be discredited and had therefore said it was an accident.

Vimochana's investigations into such cases were followed by public hearings attended by representatives of the state administration and elected representatives. The parents of some women who had died gave their testimonies at these hearings. Vimochana's findings were compared with the FIRs of these cases and the gaps and anomalies identified. Over 100 cases were reopened. A manual for police investigation of such unnatural deaths of women was prepared, with the focus on cases of burn injuries, hanging, and poisoning. The manual laid down the procedure defined by the law, including instructions on when to issue notices of inquest and whom to inform.

Vimochana's engagement with the health system was quite accidental. During the investigation, Vimochana found that most of the stove burst cases were admitted in the burn ward at Victoria Hospital in Bengaluru. Their relatives spoke about the callousness of the staff, the corruption, and the lack of hygiene on the ward.

Vimochana visited the ward and spoke to the patients and their relatives. The ward smelt strongly of burnt flesh. Women with burns lay in the corridor, almost all of them on mattresses covered in Rexine, minus sheets. Women were screaming. Relatives were crying. Patients were being asked to pay for every dressing, every change of linen, medicines, and so on. In five cases, parents reported that their daughters were administered an injection, minutes after which they gasped and died. The majority of the patients were from the lower socioeconomic strata and could not afford to seek treatment elsewhere. Vimochana documented these cases and launched a campaign on the right to die with dignity.

It organised a protest against the callousness of the staff and government, demanding that conditions at the ward be improved and corruption curbed. In response, the minister for medical education visited the hospital and announced various measures the government would take to improve conditions. Student nurses were deputed for daily dressing, bedsheets and free medicines were provided, and private staff was hired to clean the ward. Thus, Vimochana's initial campaign on women's right to live prompted it to work with the health system and health professionals to further campaign on women's right to die with dignity.

Objectives of working with the health system

Because of Vimochana's campaign, the health minister provided space for two workers from Vimochana to sit at the burn ward and monitor its functioning. They were appalled at the poorly lit and poorly ventilated ward, with unkempt and foul-smelling beds lined up in an atmosphere of passive resignation. There was utter indifference from the staff towards the women, scarred almost beyond recognition, lying groaning in pain and trauma. The lack of beds and infection control, high mortality (almost 90%), and apathy of the hospital staff were Vimochana's main concerns. Its main aim was improvement of the quality of care offered to burn patients. The interface with the police was also problematic, as they often arrived at the ward after the death of the patient or recorded statements in the presence of the husband or in-laws, taking the patient's fingerprints when they were asleep or unconscious. Often, they did not speak the language of the patient. The police even tried to convince women not to register cases and to declare the burn injuries accidental.

Approach to working with the health system

The hard questions that Vimochana asked were:

> Why was the burn ward not providing care on a par with the ICU?
> Could round-the-clock emergency care have saved precious lives?
> Were patients in the ward dying of the high degree of burns or the high degree of lethargy, apathy, and indifference?

There are two dimensions to Vimochana's work at the burn ward. One is to ensure that patients have access to quality medical care. The other is to help women and their families speak the truth and seek justice.

Access to quality medical care

Vimochana's approach to the health system is that of a watchdog (but one that barks *and* bites). It monitors on a daily basis all the functions of the ward, from cleaning, bathing, dressing, and ensuring protein-rich diets and medicines to ensuring security and free treatment for all patients. Vimochana workers have even bathed patients when professional staff were unavailable or disinterested. Vimochana follows up on medico-legal procedures, ensuring accuracy of information in medical records and recording of dying declarations. The staff interacts with patients and their families and provides counselling for both. Vimochana even raises funds to improve the quality of care.

Helping women and their families speak out

Vimochana talks to every woman at the ward from the day of admission, establishing a rapport with her and creating a safe space where she can speak out. If the woman decides to speak out and register a case, she and her family are provided legal support. Vimochana has been assisting women for more than 15 years now and is well versed in court procedures. Relatives are prepared on how to depose in court and how to deal with defence lawyers.

Women and girls who survive can attend a centre where vocational training is provided for leprosy patients. Many women have learnt to make candles, leather handbags, plastic weaves, mats, and paper bags here. Funds are raised for their travel to this centre. Group meetings with survivors facilitate mutual sharing and support.

Documentation and advocacy

Vimochana conducts detailed documentation at the hospital and presents it to the authorities periodically. This ground reporting attempts to ensure that the facilities the authorities signed up to deliver are, in fact, made available. The documentation also aims to highlight new gaps in care so that there is a constant effort to improve services for burn patients.

In addition to public protests, Vimochana has raised issues in the state legislature to build public pressure and prompt the political will to make change happen. It has been constantly reviewing existing practices, questioning whether these are adequate, identifying gaps, and demanding better standards of care.

The setting up of the Burns Development Committee in 1997 was an important step in policy advocacy. The committee comprises the state secretary of medical education, secretary planning, medical superintendent, nursing superintendent, chief medical officer, director Department of Medical Education and Research, and members of Vimochana. The role of the committee is to monitor and evaluate improvements at the ward. The committee is currently drafting a burn policy for the state health department.

Lessons from the field

Vimochana's consistent advocacy has led the state government to make some changes to conditions at the burn ward. These include:

- A separate ward for children
- Segregation of patients according to severity of burns
- Special burn diet
- Increased availability of doctors by integrating postgraduate students, house surgeons, and nursing students
- Increased availability of free medicines
- Employment of security guards to regulate the flow of visitors
- Employment of cleaners to maintain hygiene

Over the years, the government has found that the presence of Vimochana workers instils hope in patients with third-degree burns, encouraging them to record their dying declaration in an atmosphere free of fear and threat.

Vimochana also did an analysis of ten years of case records of burn patients. This study shook people up and contributed an accurate profile of burn victims. Victims were usually (i) young brides (aged 25–29 and married for less than two years) or slightly older women (aged 30 and above and married for more than eight years); (ii) Hindu; (iii) living in urban areas; (iv) living in nuclear families; and (v) housewives. In addition, they had a low level of education. The study also revealed that the majority of cases across the ten-year period were recorded falsely as accidents or suicide.

Despite all the changes introduced, however, the burn outcomes continued to be poor. Mortality remained high for most women reporting with moderate and severe burns. In the city, St John's Hospital had better burn outcomes. This highlighted the apathetic treatment of burn victims at government hospitals in comparison to private hospitals. Higher cost of care at private hospitals did seem to ensure better care. An engagement with medical professionals brought to light the inadequacy of clinical protocols at Victoria Hospital, and the need for a skin bank, better dressings, and change in surgical protocols to arrest septicaemia was raised.

Sustained advocacy has pushed the government to allocate more resources for burn care. A larger burn unit that caters to treatment, research, and prevention is being set up, and a burn policy for the state health department is being drafted. Vimochana has stressed the need for intersectoral dialogue and guidelines for each sector. From an issue perceived as one for the police to investigate, gender-based violence has come to be accepted by the health system as an issue of healthcare.

Challenges

Vimochana is one of few groups working directly with women reporting burn injuries. Despite the direct intervention, protests, campaigns, lobbying, research, and documentation, burns remain a neglected issue. Some of the challenges faced are:

- Absence of a dedicated community of doctors to save patients. This poses a big challenge in quality of care. There is a lack of interest in and apathy towards burn care due to high mortality and need for long-term treatment.
- Low priority of burn care by the health department. The establishment of a burn unit that provides the required standards of care to its patients requires substantial resources and commitment. This has been lacking, and it has taken the campaign many years to be heard.
- Absence of a comprehensive approach. The changes at the hospital have been ad hoc and slow. There is no clear policy on treatment, medico-legal care, rehabilitation, research, and prevention.
- Lack of resources in terms of staff (doctors, nurses, cleaners), medicines, and overall infrastructure.
- Lack of motivation amongst staff, especially cleaners, dressers, nurses, and even some doctors. This is the biggest impediment to provision of care. Most health providers are not interested in doing this work, as they feel the patients are going to die anyway. There is no accountability, and so they get away with negligence and ill treatment.

Recommendations and way forward

Staff training is an important way forward, and Vimochana has collaborated with Sochara to train nurses, who are the backbone of burn care. Those working in burn care should get incentives such as extra leave and rotation across wards. The good health of staff working in burn care, including good diet and adequate rest, needs priority.

So far, rehabilitation services have been ignored. There is a need to employ physiotherapists and psychologists for patients from the day of admission.

Prevention work is essential, and the public health department needs to take it up as a priority. Burns are preventable, and various measures, such as identifying areas with a high incidence of burns, creating awareness about the impact of burns and domestic violence, identifying women experiencing domestic violence at the community level, and meeting them regularly and checking on their status, are important steps. The government's move to set up one-stop crisis centres (OSCCs) in hospitals is good, but doctors and nurses need to be trained and sensitised to VAW. The OSCC staff must understand that burn injuries in women are not always accidents, and they must undertake direct work with women reporting burn injuries and provide counselling to them.

3.2 SNEHA

Nayreen Daruwalla, Preethi Pinto, and Nikhat Shaikh

SNEHA's women's OPDs at four Mumbai hospitals have complemented and strengthened the public health response to VAW.

Introduction

The Society for Nutrition, Education & Health Action (SNEHA) was set up in 1999 to cater to the many neglected problems related to the health and well-being of women and children. A group of neonatologists working at some of Mumbai's largest public hospitals launched SNEHA after observing many women from low-income communities reporting with maternal anaemia, hypertension during pregnancy, birth asphyxia, foetal distress, stillbirths, and premature or low birth weight babies. These women invariably had no financial resources to pay for their own or their child's treatment. Interviews with them revealed lack of family support and domestic violence. The violence and neglect in their homes hindered women's access to health services. SNEHA saw that the health of women and children is woven into a complex web of environmental and social deprivation, increasing their vulnerability. They saw the need to educate mothers about the importance of health-seeking behaviour during pregnancy, delivery, and the post-natal period. They also recognised the need for psychosocial support for women who face violence. This was the impetus for SNEHA's interventions. However, SNEHA was convinced from the start that their work should complement public health systems, not create parallel systems.

The Prevention of Violence against Women and Children programme began with a counselling centre for women and children in distress at the urban health centre (UHC) in Dharavi. A temporary shelter was also made available at the UHC. This is an extension centre of the Lokmanya Tilak Municipal General Hospital (LTMGH), a large tertiary hospital serving many communities in and around Dharavi, one of Asia's largest slums. With governmental and non-governmental projects on HIV, TB, and nutrition housed there, along with routine outpatient departments, it was a strategic location for SNEHA's counselling services.

A memorandum of understanding with the Mumbai Municipal Corporation allowed official space for SNEHA's counselling centre at the LTMGH extension centre as well as allotment of a few beds in the paediatric and female wards for children and women in crisis. This enabled SNEHA to coordinate with different departments in the hospital to ensure a timely response to survivors of violence. The service was intended to reinforce public infrastructure by helping create better systems of functionality and collaboration.

Approaches to working with the public health system

Health facilities are often the entry point to healthcare services for women in distress. Women who have suffered violence often present with physical and psychological complaints that are subsequently recorded as medical problems. Violence against women and girls is a violation of human rights (UN Millennium Project 2005). It also affects health and development. Domestic violence causes death (homicide, suicide, and maternal mortality) or damage through physical injury (impairment and chronic illness), emotional damage (drug and alcohol abuse, depression, and low self-esteem), sexual and reproductive ill health (unwanted pregnancy, sexually transmitted infections, HIV), and negative health behaviour (substance abuse, risk-taking) (Heise, Ellsberg, and Gottmoeller 2002).

SNEHA's programme works within Heise's socio-ecological framework of preventing violence against women, which tackles the complex interplay of factors at the individual, community, societal, and institutional level to provide primary, secondary, and tertiary interventions (Heise 1998). Volunteers help with primary prevention through group education, public campaigns, and mobile phone/online campaigns. As part of secondary and tertiary prevention, a range of psychosocial interventions are provided, such as counselling, home visits, police intervention, legal aid, and long-term counselling and support.

Over the last two decades, SNEHA has developed three major components of the programme: crisis counselling and extended response, community mobilisation, and strengthening the institutional response of public systems such as police, healthcare providers, and legal bodies.

SNEHA's work with LTMGH began with counselling and legal services for survivors of burns in the burn unit. Its counsellors visited the department thrice a week to screen and counsel survivors. They mediated with the police to file the first information report (FIR). The hospital's social work department requested SNEHA's assistance in admitting women and children to shelter facilities and looking into their repatriation. All this reaffirmed SNEHA's conviction that it is crucial to work with public health systems that provide thousands of women access to services.

There have been three ways in which SNEHA has collected data to monitor violence against women: disclosure, professional alertness, and surveys. An important way of uncovering violence is to look for it. Doctors, nurses, teachers, and community workers can read the physical signs of violence, or subtle cries for help, if they know how to interpret them (Feder et al. 2011). SNEHA believes that professionals are more likely to act if disposal is easy and does not add to their burden of responsibility. If they know whom to call, they will call.

Key components of the model

SNEHA initiated a women's OPD at LTMGH in collaboration with the forensic and psychiatry department. A crisis cell, managed by at least two SNEHA counsellors, introduced on the premises of a public hospital, has ensured timely and comprehensive crisis counselling and referrals for further action. Table 3.2.1 provides details of the nature of interventions carried out at different levels of the health system.

Formative research

In a knowledge, attitude, and perception survey carried out with 104 healthcare providers from various departments of LTMGH, 74% of healthcare providers expressed a need for a standardised protocol. Of the 78% who said there was a need for a separate cell to address gender-based violence, 52% were doctors. This clearly showed that healthcare professionals considered a response to gender-based violence through an external organisation's service important but did not perceive it as an integrated intervention of the hospital. They failed to see their role in providing support and assistance in domestic violence cases, as they considered it a private matter.

Following this survey, SNEHA conducted a formative study with the emergency medical services (EMS) and psychiatry departments to understand the epidemiology of gender-based violence. The study was on identifying women who present at psychiatry and emergency departments with emergencies and mental health conditions. It revealed that of 101 women interviewed, 54% reported a history of violence and occurrence of violence in the previous six months. Discussion of these findings with the dean and heads of various departments led to the understanding that counselling services for women and children survivors of violence at public hospitals are necessary.

Sensitising staff and building their skills

Apart from improving practical clinical skills, such as recognising the signs of GBV or documenting injuries, healthcare staff also need to understand the issues underlying GBV as well as the specific local context. The system needs to accept gender-based violence as a serious public health issue. Training efforts should not be undertaken in an isolated manner but be implemented alongside other changes in the system of care and referral (WHO 2013).

Table 3.2.1 Secondary and tertiary interventions provided by SNEHA's women's OPDs

Secondary interventions	Tertiary interventions
Domestic violence	
Counselling	Support in filing case
Support for medical intervention	Long-term counselling
Safety assessment	Psychotherapy
Registration of police complaint	Follow-up of legal case
Medico-legal support	
Home visit and family intervention	
Couple/family counselling	
Sexual assault	
Crisis counselling	Long-term counselling
Safety assessment	Follow-up with legal provisions
Accompaniment for medical examination	Follow-up for Manodhairya Scheme
Ensuring privacy and safety for examination	
Trauma counselling	
Support in recording statement	
Child sexual abuse	
Crisis counselling	Long-term counselling
Safety assessment	Follow-up with legal provisions
Accompaniment for medical examination	Follow-up with child welfare committee
Ensuring safety and privacy for medical examination	Coordination with protection officers
Coordination with police and protection officers	Follow-up for Manodhairya Scheme
Reporting to the child welfare committee	
Family counselling	
Support in recording child's statement	
Burns	
Crisis counselling	Long-term counselling
Coordination with police for filing FIR	Follow-up with investigating officer
Support in recording dying declaration	Follow-up with public prosecutor
Support in change of statement	
Interface with public prosecutor	
Family counselling	

Source: Compiled by authors.

Formation of a core group and identification of champions in the system

SNEHA requested LTMGH to nominate two staff members from each department to form a Collaborative Working Group comprising senior doctors, residents, registrars, nurses, and male and female patient attendants. All cadres of staff were engaged in a series of perspective-building and training sessions on gender, sexuality, and violence and their role as service providers. Violence is an issue that survivors may not share with doctors due to the hierarchical nature of their relationship, whereas they may find it easier to talk to nurses and support staff once a relationship is established.

Networking and building coalitions

The process of networking and building coalitions with other organisations working on the same issue ensures a multi-sectoral and coordinated response and increases efficiency in service provision. The networks may include other doctors or hospitals in the same community, government bodies such as police, and child welfare or psychosocial services as well as women's shelters or crisis centres. These networks can be used for joint advocacy for improving existing laws and policies or creating new ones. Protocols are an effective tool to specify the roles and responsibilities of different organisations involved in a coalition as well as procedures for intervention and referral (UNFPA and WAVE 2014).

Replication in other tertiary hospitals

SNEHA has initiated the women's OPDs in two other tertiary hospitals and one teaching hospital (KEM Medical College and Nair Medical College in Mumbai and Kalwa Hospital, Thane) as a full-time service, with crisis counselling and referral systems provided in coordination with different departments. This has helped in standardising protocols across all the hospitals to provide a minimum package of care.

The response to violence in women's lives is strengthened by a holistic approach that addresses women's immediate and long-term needs, recognises the emotional trauma they may suffer, and challenges the stigma that accompanies gender-based violence. The woman drives the outcomes of the intervention and counselling, as SNEHA puts the woman's agency and right to choose at the centre of its work. Once the survivor is certain about availing services from the centre, an intake sheet records the survivor's consent and interventions are provided in accordance with the choices she makes.

While dealing with domestic violence cases, SNEHA has learnt that constant interaction with doctors on duty is necessary to ensure documentation of injuries for evidence creation. To ensure that the woman learns to recognise violence, negotiate effectively, and break the cycle of violence, long-term interventions with the woman and others involved are necessary.

SNEHA's observations while dealing with sexual assault cases have been that doctors follow protocols but not every doctor handles the case sensitively. Effective medical treatment is always provided, but the age of the survivor determines the level of empathy displayed by the doctor. Doctors show a lot of empathy for survivors aged 1–12 years, whereas in the 12- to 15-year age bracket, empathy depends on how the assault has taken place. If a child aged 15–18 is in a consensual relationship, the responsibility for the act is placed upon the child. There is much emphasis on the breaking of the hymen for girls aged 12 and above. In burn cases, the protocols for medical treatment and lodging a medico-legal complaint are well defined by the system. Generally, arrangements are made for a change of statement to be recorded as and when the survivor wishes. However, there is ambiguity in recording a dying declaration, as often the responsibility is shifted to the police officer. In such instances, death occurs without recording a dying declaration.

In addition to referring cases to hospitals, SNEHA gets referrals from the hospital. If, in the course of treatment, physicians recognise that a patient needs counselling or is a survivor of violence, they write a note and refer them to the women's OPD. The counsellors keep the doctor in the loop throughout the subsequent intervention, which includes social investigation, counselling, legal support, rehabilitation, and providing shelter if necessary. Based on the survivor's consent, counsellors call the perpetrator and necessary family members for counselling.

Since inception, 7,495 cases have been registered at all the women's OPDs. Seventy-five percent of them have been of intimate partner violence and domestic violence, 15% of sexual violence, and 10% child sexual abuse cases registered under POCSO.

Achievements of the model

Initially, SNEHA faced much resistance from doctors and health officials; people doubted the role of an NGO like SNEHA in the health sector. The hospital did not understand the organisation's motivations or its efforts to help them comprehend issues of gender-based violence. Over time, they saw the value of helping women and children access the hospital. Now, the public hospitals have come to understand SNEHA's role in the public health ecosystem, from facilitating legal services, filing FIRs for survivors, and intervening in the community to coordinating with the police. They have accepted SNEHA as a part of the hospital (though not formally), and at LTMGH the counsellor is allowed to add a comment on the survivor's case paper in cases of sexual assault and child sexual abuse. This has been a small milestone in SNEHA's progress.

The work with the burn department has helped women file FIRs and legal cases. Additionally, the work with the psychiatry department has evolved from help with social interventions to psychological counselling, and this department currently refers the maximum number of cases to the SNEHA counselling centre at LTMGH.

SNEHA's relationship with the formal health system has become more of a partnership through the women's OPDs. Data and reflections on trends and concerns are shared with the dean of the hospital to improve screening policies and interventions. SNEHA continues to formalise its work with the health sector, setting up a system of case auditing in which all departments that have coordinated on a particular case review and evaluate the holistic nature of the response and intervention.

Training has been an important activity carried out by SNEHA at all the hospitals it works with. In 2018, SNEHA conducted 48 training sessions for 1,175 healthcare workers on gender, violence, and health; 22 trainings with 904 nurses; and nine trainings with 542 nursing students.

SNEHA's initiative has worked towards making violence against women a public health concern. Public health systems and community members recognise SNEHA as not only a credible service-provisioning organisation but also an advocate for effective systems and processes to respond to and prevent violence against women and children.

The biggest impact has been the strengthening of the health sector response to VAW, with 62% of cases seen at the counselling centre now being referred by healthcare professionals from local hospitals. In 2018, 914 survivors of violence (716 women and 198 children) received support from women's OPDs in all four hospitals. Of these, healthcare providers referred as many as 762 cases (83%).

While SNEHA had once observed that doctors were reluctant to get involved in legal procedures, now, when SNEHA intervenes and supports the doctors in recording the dying declaration, they are more likely to write it.

SNEHA has followed CEHAT's Dilaasa model for its women's OPDs within the health system. As with Dilaasa, in the long term the women's OPDs should be fully integrated with the public health system, with the state government or municipal corporation funding and running them.

Major challenges

The sustainability of the programme continues to be a challenge. Presently, SNEHA mobilises resources to run the women's OPDs, but eventually these costs need to be integrated into hospital budgets. In addition, an overburdened health system may not see gender-based violence as integral to its work. Lack of infrastructure, stringent administrative frameworks, and the high doctor-patient ratio are a real concern for sustainability and limit the system from taking leadership and building accountability.

Institutionalising training on gender-based violence for healthcare providers is another challenge.

Coordination between the departments of gynaecology, forensics, and medical and social work has improved after the implementation of the POCSO Act, 2012. They have understood the NGO's role in providing immediate psychosocial support and evidence-building. The counsellor's observations are recorded on the inhouse medical case sheet. To sustain the work, it is important to build leaders or champions within the system who will take the work forward. However, the different stakeholders within the system continue to see their roles as separate from one another. There is no coordination between the police and healthcare providers, for instance. SNEHA's efforts to improve documentation have received a slower response, as the healthcare system has no faith in the legal system and is worried it may have to depose and come to court repeatedly if it intervenes. The forensics department complains of delays caused by the taking of unnecessary swabs, and the police and health system blame the legal system for negating all their efforts by releasing perpetrators on bail for lack of evidence. At LTMG Hospital, with which SNEHA has the longest association, there is considerable improvement in synchronisation of work on cases of sexual violence. SNEHA is contacted in each case, and its notes are included in the official hospital documents.

In spite of all these concerns, SNEHA believes that hospitals are the best place for programmes such as Nirbhaya Centres and women's OPDs.

References

Feder, G et al. (2011): "Identification and Referral to Improve Safety (IRIS) of women experiencing domestic violence with a primary care training and support programme: A cluster randomised controlled trial," *The Lancet*, Vol 378, No 9805, pp. 1788–1795.

Heise, L (1998): "Violence against women: An integrated, ecological framework," *Violence against Women*, Vol 4, No 3, pp. 262–290.

Heise, L, Ellsberg, M and Gottmoeller, M (2002): "A global overview of gender-based violence," *International Journal of Gynecology & Obstetrics*, Vol 78, p. S1.

UNFPA and WAVE (2014): *Strengthening health system responses to gender-based violence in Eastern Europe and Central Asia: A resource package*, Istanbul: United Nations Population Fund and Vienna, WAVE.

UN Millennium Project (2005): *Taking action: Achieving gender equality and empowering women*, Task Force on Education and Gender Equality, United Nations Development Programme and Earthscan, published by Earthscan in the UK and USA in 2005.

WHO (2013): *Global and regional estimates of violence against women: Prevalence and health effects of intimate partner violence and non-partner sexual violence*, Geneva: World Health Organization.

3.3 Soukhya

Suneeta Krishnan, N S Vishwanath, Prarthana Appaiah, Anuradha Sreevathsa, Nayanatara Patil, Kameshwari Devi, Sangeeta Rege, and Padma Bhate-Deosthali

The Soukhya project in Bengaluru demonstrates that primary health centres can become safe spaces for the disclosure of domestic violence and care of survivors.[1]

Introduction

The staggeringly high prevalence of domestic violence (physical, psychological, or sexual violence perpetrated by husbands or other marital family members) in India and the related adverse health impacts have been extensively documented over several decades. In Bengaluru, a longitudinal study by the St John's Medical College conducted with 747 young (aged 16–25 years) married women revealed that nearly 80% had experienced domestic violence since marriage (Rocca et al. 2009). Two deaths among this cohort of women, attributed to domestic violence, further highlighted the urgent need for interventions to prevent and respond to the adverse consequences of domestic violence. This was the starting point of the effort to develop and evaluate a primary healthcare response to domestic violence in Bengaluru, which is the focus of this chapter.

Healthcare-based responses to domestic violence

Research elsewhere in the world has highlighted that healthcare settings are important entry points for interventions that seek to prevent intimate partner violence and related adverse health outcomes (Chibber and Krishnan 2011). As part of the longitudinal study in Bengaluru, the St John's Medical College conducted qualitative research with women experiencing domestic violence and public and private sector primary healthcare providers to explore the potential for a primary healthcare response in Bengaluru (Chibber, Krishnan, and Minkler 2011). The study found that primary healthcare centres could offer an acceptable and safe space for disclosure and discussion of domestic violence (Chibber, Krishnan, and Minkler 2011). Women emphasised the following elements of a primary healthcare-based domestic violence response: trust in the primary care provider built through familiarity and a long-standing relationship; confidence that the provider is in a position to help; and belief that a provider-initiated enquiry about domestic conflict and violence raises awareness about domestic violence as a health issue. Interviews with healthcare providers highlighted the importance of training and role models to improve providers' skills in responding to violence and addressing gender inequitable attitudes. Providers underscored the importance of having strong referral linkages, guidelines for responding to domestic violence, and a system-level commitment (demonstrated through policies and standard operating protocols) to addressing domestic violence as a health issue.

Women's utilisation of healthcare services, particularly antenatal care, maternal care, and child health services, has increased substantially in India during the last two decades (Chibber and Krishnan 2011). This is at least in part due to increased investment following the declaration of the Millennium Development Goals (MDGs). The Soukhya project, the joint initiative of the St John's Medical College and Bengaluru Municipal Corporation, sought to capitalise on these trends and develop a primary healthcare response to domestic violence in Bengaluru. The project drew inspiration and insights from Indian and global experiences of healthcare-based responses to domestic violence. Two specific programmes that guided Soukhya's work included the crisis centre response pioneered by CEHAT at a municipal hospital in Mumbai (Bhate-Deosthali, Ravindran, and Vindhya 2012) and the systems approach developed by the Kaiser Permanente Family Clinics in California (McCaw and Kotz 2005). The overall goal of the Soukhya project, launched in 2011, was to develop and assess the acceptability, feasibility, and potential effectiveness of a municipal primary healthcare system intervention to respond to domestic violence.

Working with the Bengaluru municipal health system

The development of the health system response was based on findings from the aforementioned research as well as discussions with the municipal health system (administrators and healthcare providers) and other key stakeholders (health experts, domestic violence–related service providers, and researchers). An iterative, participatory process was used to engage with these stakeholders. A programme advisory group was formed, comprising the joint commissioner of health, the chief health officer, and representatives from the three cadres of healthcare workers: physicians, nurses, and community link workers. Roundtables were held with members of this group as well as other stakeholders to define the components of the intervention, draft protocols and training curricula, and develop job aids. Based on a mapping of referral organisations, a network was established to bring together agencies offering shelter, legal aid, counselling, and other services. Discussions with network members led to the identification of referral mechanisms. Periodic meetings have been held with all constituents since the launch of the initiative.

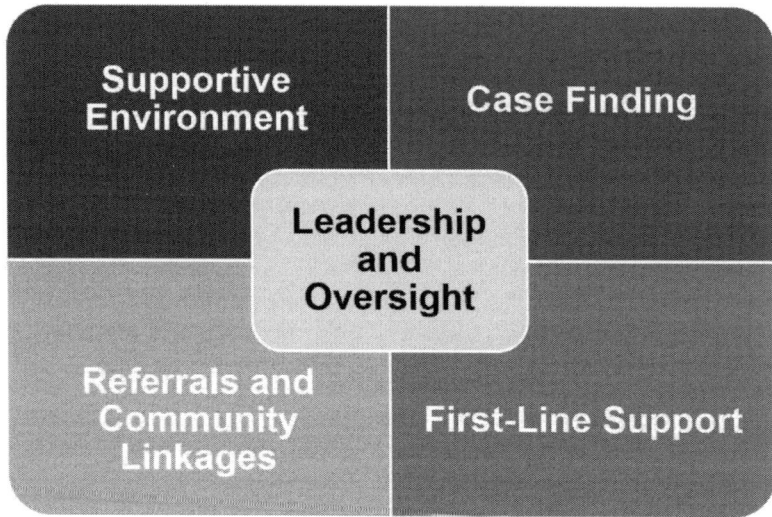

Figure 3.3.1 Soukhya intervention components
Source: Compiled by authors.

The Soukhya intervention had five components aimed at a comprehensive, health system–based response to domestic violence (Figure 3.3.1): case-finding, first-line support, community linkages, supportive environment, and leadership. Data collection and analysis were integral to the intervention. Periodic surveys of healthcare providers and women using primary healthcare services and qualitative interviews documented implementation of the initiative and assessed outcomes.

In the first phase of Soukhya, between 2011 and 2013, the project worked with healthcare providers (physicians, nurses, and link workers) in 54 primary health centres in two of the three core zones of the Bengaluru Municipal Corporation. In the second phase (2013–16), the project focused on 20 primary health centres.

Intervention components

Case-finding

Case-finding is essentially a provider-led enquiry on domestic conflict and violence that can lead to women's disclosure of violence. The protocol for case-finding was developed in a participatory fashion. A two-day residential retreat with members of the programme advisory group and other experts helped develop the training modules that would equip healthcare providers with the knowledge and skills to engage in case-finding and other aspects of the intervention.

At the end of the workshop, two eight-hour in-service training modules emerged – one for nurses and physicians and the other for link workers. Topics addressed in these modules included gender roles, inequities and gender-based violence, patriarchy, the health impact of violence, role of healthcare providers, and legal and other available services.

Case-finding was initially limited to physicians and nurses and was integrated into routine primary healthcare provision. Case identification was typically initiated using indirect questions in response to triggers. Triggers could include reports of tiredness and exhaustion, inability to negotiate family planning, delayed childhood immunisation, or other signs and symptoms. Indirect questioning served to establish a rapport with the woman. It also provided a rationale for eventually posing more direct questions on the domestic conflict and violence that contribute to the health problem. The goal of the case-finding process was to raise awareness among women that domestic conflict and violence contribute to adverse health outcomes and to provide an opening for disclosure.

A reference for case identification (in the form of a desktop job aid), which described common triggers encountered in antenatal, prenatal, family planning, and immunisation clinics – as well as other clinics – and examples of indirect and direct questions, was given to all providers. The training emphasised the critical importance of ensuring privacy and confidentiality during the identification process through discussions and role-play.

First-line support

The second component of the intervention was first-line support, which is the response that is to be provided to all women who disclose violence. Although the project initially envisioned physicians and nurses as the main implementers of first-line support, we found that women often disclosed (unprompted) violence to community link workers. As a result, all cadres of healthcare workers were trained to offer first-line support. Support may also be provided to women who may not disclose violence but show signs of it. This brief protocol involves provision of essential knowledge on women's rights as well as support services (linkages and referrals) available through the health centre and a safety-planning component.

First-line support involves:

- Building rapport through empathetic, non-judgemental responses and eye contact and establishing privacy and safety
- Ensuring privacy and confidentiality when implementing first-line support and follow-up interactions; for example, arranging a meeting with the woman at the health centre if disclosure occurs in the community
- Reinforcing key messages, including an acknowledgement of women's situation, and providing information on women's right to live a violence-free life, including key provisions of the Protection of Women from Domestic Violence Act (PWDVA)

- Developing a personalised safety plan to remain safe in their relationship
- Providing information on and assessing the need for support services such as shelter

The first-line support protocol was distributed to all providers in the form of a small booklet in Kannada, the local language, or English. A directory of referral services as well as a format for documenting disclosure and referrals was also provided.

Community linkages

The third component, community linkages, was promoted through outreach by link workers and through the referral network. Link workers were tasked with raising awareness of domestic violence as a health issue and linking women to the health centre during routine community outreach programmes (mothers' meetings, for example) and home visits. Talking points in the form of a booklet and scripts were developed as tools to ensure standardisation of messages. Link workers were also encouraged to engage with community-based women's groups and to enlist their support in raising awareness.

Health centre staff – nurses and physicians – were positioned to link women to support services through the referral network. Soukhya sought to bring a range of organisations providing different services to women experiencing violence under one umbrella. The goal was to increase the chances that women would get the services they need when they need them. The services included counselling, short stay, childcare, legal aid, and vocational training. After multiple iterations, considering the ease of access, feedback from providers and women, organisational visits, and the organisation's interest in being part of the initiative, a functional and active referral network coalesced. Regular meetings (at least twice a year) were held to discuss challenges and improve service provision. Referrals were made using a standard referral form with de-identified information in duplicate and the process was documented in a separate register maintained by the physician.

Supportive environment

Establishing a supportive environment within the clinic was the fourth component of the programme. A supportive environment included ensuring a safe space for disclosure – by emphasising privacy and confidentiality, offering women choices and corresponding decisions, and providing opportunities for disclosure. Informative posters encouraged women to talk to their healthcare provider about domestic violence. A poster for health centre staff highlighted their responsibility in addressing domestic violence. Job aids emphasised the importance of ensuring privacy and confidentiality as part of the response to violence.

Leadership and oversight

The fifth and final component of the intervention was leadership and oversight. Soukhya collaborated with champions within the municipal system – physicians identified over the course of the research as already responding to domestic violence – to foster ownership and leadership as well as mechanisms for monitoring and longer-term sustainability. Two members of the team – a physician and a social worker who have collaborated with the municipal health department for many years – focused specifically on advocacy.

The advocacy efforts focused on municipal administrators and municipal healthcare providers who were sceptical of the need for and feasibility of the intervention. They organised visits and interactions with representatives of funding agencies, experts, and community-based organisations. The Soukhya team, together with the champions within the municipal system, presented data from their research and case studies from within the Bengaluru municipal health system.

To ensure sustainability of the intervention, Soukhya pushed for a memorandum of understanding with the municipal corporation to integrate the effort into the existing health programme and to adopt a city-level action plan to address domestic violence and its health impacts.

Experiences of implementation

Outcomes

In the first phase, between 2011 and 2013, Soukhya completed face-to-face training of healthcare providers (physicians, nurses, and link workers) at 54 primary health centres in two of the three core zones of the Bengaluru Municipal Corporation. Toolkits, including a protocol, case-finding aid, referral directory, posters, scripts, and a booklet with talking points, were developed and distributed.

There was wide variation in case-finding, with a handful of doctors, nurses, and link workers being the most active. In the majority of cases, case-finding led to the delivery of first-line support, with little additional follow-up. Eighty cases were identified and referred to the project counsellors over an 18-month period. The majority of women who were referred were provided counselling via phone or face-to-face, and 19 women requested referrals to shelters, legal aid, police, or alcohol de-addiction services. Three women registered cases under the PWDVA with the help of referral organisations and one pursued a divorce. Overall, documentation of activities was minimal, with the only reliable data on service provision being the referrals made to the project counsellors.

Surveys with healthcare providers indicated that knowledge of domestic violence (specifically, the forms of violence), its health impact, and the role of healthcare providers improved after training but was not necessarily sustained. Exit interviews with women revealed that they were more likely to have been asked about domestic conflict and violence and to be aware of different forms of violence after the healthcare providers' training.

In the second phase of the initiative (2013–16), Soukhya focused on 20 health centres. After several meetings with the top leadership of the municipal corporation, the advocacy efforts began to produce results. Sustained advocacy (as well as media coverage of the Nirbhaya case) culminated in the appointment of a municipal health department champion as nodal officer for domestic violence prevention and response. The nodal officer has been an integral part of the team, supporting refresher trainings, conducting supervisory visits, monitoring progress, and advocating for mainstreaming of services within the municipal health system.

The health department mandated reporting on the number of women reached with messages on domestic violence and the number of women who had disclosed domestic violence and been supported. Approximately 80% of the health centres (16 of 20) have been submitting reports on a monthly basis. These data are reviewed by the nodal officer and discussed at the monthly meetings of healthcare providers. Following the introduction of the National Urban Health Mission in Bengaluru, the project team was invited to train newly recruited ASHAs.

Challenges

The Soukhya initiative has experienced numerous challenges, the majority of which have been at the system level. In the initial years, there was lack of recognition by the municipal administration of domestic violence as a health issue (it was seen as a private household matter). Although this changed over time, domestic violence continues to be a relatively low-priority problem for the administration. Building a case for a domestic violence response was difficult because key officials such as the commissioner, joint commissioner for health, and chief health officer frequently changed following transfers or retirement. Bureaucratic procedures often delayed decision-making, with all decisions (from approvals for training sessions to the memorandum of understanding) being subjected to multiple steps and involvement of a number of officials.

Capacity-building efforts were limited by the pressures of existing programmes, leaving little time for providers, especially physicians, to participate in trainings. In addition, even within the three cadres of healthcare providers there was considerable staff turnover. The municipal system typically has fewer physicians than needed to staff all primary health centres, so the existing physicians tend to be saddled with clinical and administrative duties. Recruitment has been hampered by the many alternative (better paid) opportunities to practice in Bengaluru. Nursing staff were the most stable cadre, but they also juggle many responsibilities. Link workers, the closest to women in the community, and in many instances the most visible municipal health staff, were also the least motivated. They were retained as contract workers and paid irregularly, sometimes going six months without pay. Thus, although most providers acknowledged domestic violence as a health and women's rights issue after the training, the motivation to address the problem remained low. The problem was exacerbated by the impending introduction of the National Urban Health Mission, with its own staffing structure, further destabilising the existing staff.

Some other factors further impeded the provision of first-line support and community linkages. Organisations explicitly focused on providing domestic violence-related services are scarce. Other than shelters, the team had diffi-culty finding service providers for counselling and legal aid, particularly those that could be readily accessed by women. Feminist counselling, an approach that has been long advocated for by CEHAT and which Soukhya has found to be fundamental to a domestic violence response, is not practiced by most organisations that offer counselling. The few women who wanted to avail themselves of provisions under the PWDVA faced numerous obstacles even when highly motivated to pursue this course of action. There are very few individuals or organisations providing free legal services. Even when lawyers are willing to offer free services, cases may not move forward because of the complexity of the process, lack of consistent engagement by lawyers, and demotivation of clients. Building linkages across governmental agencies has also been challenging because of frequent leadership changes. Thus, even if health system challenges can be overcome, an effective response will be possible only if intersectoral linkages are present, functional, and effective.

Reflections

The Soukhya project in Bengaluru has demonstrated that a primary health-care response implemented through the public health system is feasible and acceptable. The support of the municipal administration was secured through consistent advocacy. The project successfully trained healthcare providers; initiated case-finding, provision of first-line support, and com-munity linkages; and established a reporting and oversight mechanism. To date, no adverse consequences as a result of the domestic violence response have emerged. The hypothesis that primary health centres can be safe spaces for disclosure and that disclosure will be facilitated through a case-finding approach has been supported (although it is difficult to prove because there are no data for the period before our programme was put in place). Exit interviews with women have suggested that trust and confidence in the abil-ity of primary healthcare providers to support women experiencing violence increased after the intervention.

However, the quality of the response is far from satisfactory. Firstly, system-level challenges, such as consistent leadership, improvements in human resources, and human resource practices, and accountability need to be addressed. In the absence of structural improvements, the domestic violence response across health centres is inconsistent. Domestic violence as a health issue needs to be prioritised. A national- or state-level policy addressing domestic violence as a health issue would help.

Secondly, the community linkage component needs improvement. Link workers (now replaced by ASHAs at centres that have been selected to implement the National Health Mission programme) require tools to support communication around domestic violence and health in the community. Communication messages and strategies to address gender-based violence and its impact on community health should be tested for effectiveness before being converted into tools.

Moreover, a coordinated response to the provision of support services is called for. Soukhya was inspired by the decades-old San Francisco Domestic Violence Consortium (interestingly, San Francisco is Bengaluru's sister city) and attempted to develop a similar platform through its referral network. However, establishing a robust network calls for an array of organisations providing the needed services, a willingness to work together in a coordinated way, and resources to support a dedicated effort. These conditions have not yet coalesced in Bengaluru.

Thirdly, more mechanisms to gather evidence and assess the short- and longer-term outcomes of a health system–led response to domestic violence need to be developed. Mobile technology is promising and should be explored.

In conclusion, although Soukhya has demonstrated that a primary healthcare response is feasible and acceptable, the challenge in the future is to create a measurable, high-quality, effective, and sustainable response.

Note

1 We acknowledge with gratitude the partnership and efforts of front-line healthcare providers, community health workers, and health department staff of the Bengaluru Municipal Corporation and numerous other organisations and agencies to establish a response to violence against women. This work was supported by grants from the Indian Council of Medical Research (ICMR) and the United States Agency for International Development (USAID). The views expressed here are solely those of the authors.

References

Bhate-Deosthali, P, Ravindran, T K S and Vindhya, U (2012): "Addressing domestic violence in healthcare settings," *Economic and Political Weekly*, Vol 47, No 17, pp. 66–75.

Chibber, K S and Krishnan, S (2011): "Confronting intimate partner violence: A global health priority," *Mt Sinai Journal of Medicine*, Vol 78, No 3, pp. 449–457.

Chibber, K S, Krishnan, S and Minkler, M (2011): "Physician practices in response to intimate partner violence in Southern India: Insights from a qualitative study," *Women & Health*, Vol 51, No 2, pp. 168–185.

McCaw, B and Kotz, K (2005): "Family violence prevention program: Another way to save a life," *The Permanente Journal*, Vol 9, No 1, pp. 65–68.

Rocca, C H et al. (2009): "Challenging assumptions about women's empowerment: Social and economic resources and domestic violence among young married women in urban South India," *International Journal of Epidemiology*, Vol 38, No 2, pp. 577–585.

3.4 SWATI

Poonam Kathuria, Anagha Pradhan, and Jasodra Rana

SWATI's crisis cell at a hospital in rural Gujarat makes rural health delivery systems responsive to VAW.

Introduction

The prevention of violence against women is the primary objective of the Society for Women's Action and Training Initiatives (SWATI), which works in Gujarat for the attainment of women's rights and entitlements. SWATI aims to empower women to combat VAW, challenging community mindsets and working to make the criminal justice system – the police and judiciary – responsive to VAW. Since SWATI works primarily with rural women, the organisation began to think about ways to influence rural institutions that could change community attitudes and aid in early detection and prevention of VAW. SWATI began by looking at violence as a governance concern that could be addressed by gram panchayats. The other institution SWATI focused on is the rural health delivery mechanism. This was born of SWATI's understanding that women's poor health is also a consequence of their secondary social status and the violence to which they are continually subjected.

In 2002, SWATI set up Mahila Nyaya Panchayats (MNPs) in four blocks of Patan and Surendranagar districts as women-led gender-just platforms that equip women to combat VAW. SWATI observed the difficulty members of the MNPs experienced with the health system as they struggled to access the medical reports of women with VAW-related injuries from government hospitals and realised how important it is to work with the healthcare delivery system to address VAW.

In 2008, SWATI got the opportunity to document CEHAT's work on the Dilaasa model, and this provided the perspective and approach for SWATI's crisis intervention and support cell at a rural community health and referral hospital in Gujarat.

Process of setting up the cell

District Patan was selected because it is a remote rural area where SWATI has a strong field presence. Radhanpur, where the cell is located, is one of two administrative blocks (the other being Santalpur) where SWATI has been working on the right to information (RTI) and the setting up of MNPs. In terms of human development indicators, the two blocks are remotely located and poor and have some of the most socially and culturally backward populations.

Setting up the intervention, support, and counselling cell in a rural tertiary care hospital was a prolonged process. While it was easy to convince the senior bureaucracy of the logic and importance of a cell in a hospital setting, several bureaucrats felt it would pose an additional burden on an already over-stretched public health system. One senior bureaucrat candidly said, "They should first do what they are supposed to do," the implication being that addressing VAW is not the primary responsibility of the public health system. It took SWATI two years to get permission from the state government to set up a cell at the Radhanpur referral and community health centre. The cell was to be run jointly by the hospital and SWATI, with the hospital providing suitable space and SWATI building the capacity of the hospital staff. Launched on July 10, 2012, the cell is the first of its kind in the state of Gujarat and is perhaps the first formal rural health system initiative in the country jointly undertaken by the Department of Public Health and Family Welfare, Government of Gujarat, and an NGO specifically working on VAW and health.

The 80-bed community health centre (CHC)–cum-referral hospital in Radhanpur has an emergency unit, and a trauma care centre has been built recently. The hospital caters to three blocks around Radhanpur. The outpatient department (OPD) sees about 200 patients a day.

The hospital superintendent was receptive to the idea of the cell, facilitating a meeting with the staff, which was held after hospital hours and attended by 35 medical staffers. The response of the staff was positive, and it was only after they agreed to support the cell that SWATI approached the Government of Gujarat about setting up a joint initiative at the Radhanpur hospital.

Defining the roles of hospital and NGO

The permission letter from the government clearly stated that the hospital and SWATI would run the cell jointly, with SWATI undertaking training of the hospital staff. The hospital was extremely short-staffed at the time (50% of posts filled), so there was no way their staff could be deputed to the cell. The centre began functioning with a SWATI staffer as counsellor.

Orientation and capacity-building of hospital-based healthcare providers

In the initial period, the focus was on gaining acceptance and training and sensitising the hospital staff. Between 2012 and 2013, SWATI conducted eight trainings for the entire staff on gender-based violence as a public health issue and the sociological factors underlying VAW (Box 3.4.1).

Box 3.4.1 Topics included for training by SWATI

1   Why public health services are important in violence prevention
2   Orientation to violence against women
3   Gender-based discrimination
4   Patriarchy
5   Health impact of VAW on women and role of public health system
6   Identification of VAW
7   Building an enabling environment for women (in the hospital)
8   Referral and record maintenance

Development of print media for awareness generation

SWATI developed printed reference material, including a handbook on the role of healthcare providers in preventing VAW, a guide for counsellors on the ethics of counselling on VAW, and different pamphlets and posters for hospital- and community-based health staff. It also reached out to patients (potential clients). Posters and banners publicising the services provided at the cell were displayed at several places in the hospital. Publicity pamphlets were distributed to OPD patients.

Establishing feedback and reporting mechanisms within the hospital

Hospital authorities were periodically provided information on the functioning of the cell and the additional support they could extend to the women. They were also provided feedback on cases referred by them.

Orientation and sensitisation of PHC/village-level staff

In addition to counselling and guidance for VAW survivors detected amongst the patients approaching the hospital, the cell also strove for early detection and referral through community-level healthcare providers. SWATI conducted orientation trainings of ASHAs and regularly followed up with them during their monthly meetings. Remotely located and scattered health personnel were sent voice messages on mobile phones to create and reinforce awareness about the health impact of VAW, the role they could play, and the address of the cell.

Setting up a multi-agency support system

Survivors of VAW need multiple services to be free of violence and abuse and to be rehabilitated with dignity and rights. This includes police, legal aid, shelter home services, and staff to negotiate with the community. This kind of multi-agency response is not available in rural areas. SWATI has been working through the MNP platforms for follow-up, home visits, help with police and shelter homes, and mediation with the community, including extended family and members and leaders of the caste panchayats.

Sustainability of the cell

Since initiation, SWATI has worked to build ownership of the cell amongst hospital authorities. Monthly reports and feedback to the administration ensured transparency. Systematic documentation of cases addressed, monitoring of quality of counselling, and periodic assessment of the impact of the cell help generate evidence that will prove useful for advocacy with the public health system and replication of the model.

Utilisation of services offered

The cell began getting referrals within a month of the orientation for healthcare providers from the hospital. Between July 2012 and February 2015, referrals from hospital staff accounted for 48% (109/227) of all referrals. Other sources of referral (52%, 118/227) include old patients and ASHAs (Figure 3.4.1).

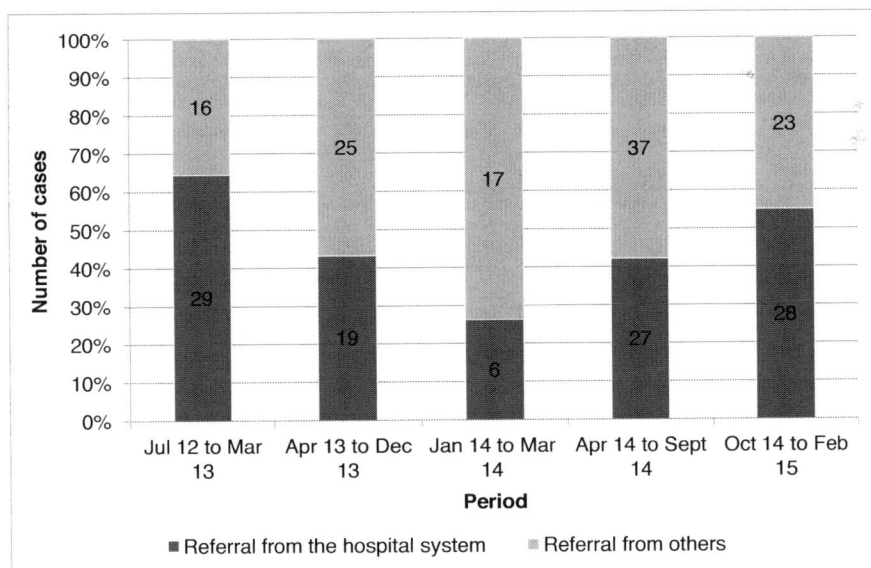

Figure 3.4.1 Number of cases and sources of referral to SWATI
Source: Compiled by authors.

Figure 3.4.2 presents the nature of injury for the 69 "severe injury" cases referred to the cell by the casualty department of the hospital. Over one-third of these (39%, 27/69) were cases of sexual assault and injury.

Analysis of a sub-sample

Analysis of a random sub-sample of 79 cases shows that almost half (48%, 38/79) the women had travelled up to 10 km to reach the cell and another 47% (37/79) had travelled up to 50 km, while 5% (4/79) had travelled up to 130 km.

The distribution of cases by sources of referral to the centre highlights the importance of a multi-pronged approach for a rural model. One-fourth of the cases (26%, 20/79) had been referred by old clients – women who had approached the cell seeking a solution to their own problems. Another 25% (19/79) were referred by community-level support structures such as ASHAs, Mahila Nyaya Panchayats, and paralegal workers. Healthcare providers from the hospital where the crisis cell is situated had referred 24% (19/79). There were referrals from other stakeholders and potential support structures as well, such as police, lawyers, community leaders, and other NGOs. This distribution of cases from different sources of referral is indicative of the importance of working at multiple levels – tertiary hospital,

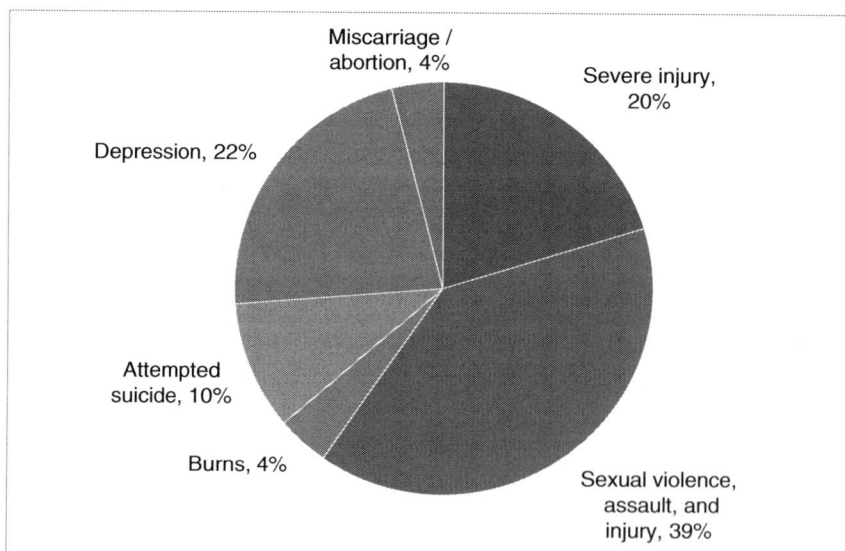

Figure 3.4.2 Nature of health complaints (n = 69) reported to SWATI

Source: Compiled by authors.

Note: Data are for the period April 2013 to February 2014.

community-based support structures, and formal institutions, the police, lawyers, and the judiciary.

The high proportion of referrals from community-level actors, including old cases, suggests that violence against women is acknowledged and discussed at the community level and indicates the potential for creating a support structure for, and a system of, getting information and guidance to violence survivors at the community level. Any initiative that succeeds in this would find success in preventing VAW or preventing the escalation of violence.

Analysis of the main reason for approaching the counsellor shows that 46% (36/79) of the women sought advice on what they could do to escape violence at home. The other 54% (43/79), however, had very clear ideas on the intervention they needed. They sought legal support (13%, 10/79), divorce (10%, 8/79), and filing a police case (10%, 8/79) or claim to property and land (9%, 7/79). This also demonstrates the need for a centre accessible to women.

Analysis of this sub-sample also validates the multi-agency approach. In 51% (50/78) of cases, the Mahila Nyaya Panchayat was involved, indicating the need for legal guidance for women. In an almost equal proportion of cases (49%, 38/78), the counsellor reached out to the woman's family members to explore whether they could ensure the support the client needed until her problem was resolved. Involvement of the police (30%, 23/79) and doctors (26%, 20/79) in more than one-fourth of the cases reiterates the need for strong linkages with formal systems.

Though the cases in this sub-sample had been with the counsellor for differing periods, data indicate that in extreme cases the counsellor may be required to hold as many as 20 meetings with the woman. Most (67%, 52/78) cases, however, required up to three meetings with the counsellor.

A telephone helpline initiated in January 2015 has received an encouraging response. Within the first month, the helpline received 32 enquiries and conducted 19 phone counsellings.

Challenges

1   Intensive sensitisation and training of community-based health workers for identification and referral of cases call for regular follow-up through personal contact, voice messaging, and other means.
2   A survivor may need several levels of intervention, all of which the cell workers may not be able to undertake. Therefore, a multi-agency supportive referral system needs to be identified and enabled.
3   Support facilities, such as psychiatric care and shelter homes, may be located at distant places.
4   The rural social context is much more community-based than urban centres. Often, therefore, the cell is dealing with the entire community, not just the survivor and her immediate family. The issues that come to the cell are much more complex, as they involve customary practices

of child marriage, exchange marriage, and a complete taboo on separation or marrying outside one's caste.

5   Shortage of medical staff because trained professionals do not want to come to rural areas.

Next steps

SWATI has successfully laid the groundwork for the cell's functioning. It now aims to set up an evidence-based proof of concept model that can be demonstrated to governments for rural areas. During the next two years, SWATI would like to:

- Streamline the functioning of the cell as a system and structure suitable to rural referral hospitals
- Conduct studies and develop an evidence-based model that can be replicated
- Develop capacity-building manuals for field-level health personnel
- Develop a module with audio material for holistic training of staff at various levels of the hospital system as well as field staff and staff at the cell
- Strengthen the referral, support, and follow-up system by setting up a service unit, either with the MNP or with another service provider in the area

3.5 Anweshi

K Ajitha, P Sreeja, and Jayalakshmi Rajeev

Anweshi's healthcare centre for survivors of violence, adjacent to Medical College Hospital, Kozhikode, has succeeded in sensitising healthcare professionals to VAW but illustrates the difficulties in integrating interventions within the public health system.

Introduction

K Ajitha and a group of women activists, advocates, social workers, doctors, psychologists, and homemakers set up Anweshi in November 1993. It began work as the Anweshi Women's Counselling Centre, which aimed to support women suffering from different types of violence. Anweshi was inspired by the work of Bodhana (meaning "awareness"), a Kozhikode-based organisation in the late 1980s that dealt with domestic violence, especially dowry deaths, forming action committees to draw attention to cases of violence reported in the media. These activities and experiences later helped the founders of Anweshi formulate the working strategy of Anweshi.

Anweshi, based in Kozhikode district, serves almost all the districts of North Kerala (Kozhikode, Kannur, Malappuram, Kasargod, and Wayanad), covering both rural and urban areas. In the initial years, Anweshi provided psychological support and counselling for women experiencing violence. Then, realising that psychological counselling by itself is not enough to resist violence, it began working towards the economic and political empowerment of survivors, providing comprehensive services to women of all age groups who suffer domestic violence, rape, sexual harassment, child abuse, and trafficking. As a long-term objective, Anweshi works for the individual, social, economic, and political empowerment of women so that they can fight violence with courage. Anweshi enables survivors of violence to make informed decisions for themselves rather than forcing a solution upon them.

In Kerala, violence against women, especially domestic violence, is still considered a family issue, one that needs to be sorted out privately within the household. Stigmatising societal attitudes and interminable delays in the judicial system ensure that most families do not report rape either. Anweshi strives to change this attitude and create awareness that VAW is a public issue that must get more attention and accountability from society. It also tries to convince women that violence is not their fault and that they deserve a better life.

Approaches to dealing with violence against women and children

Counselling

In January 2000, the Anweshi Women's Support and Advocacy Centre was set up and the project was expanded to provide legal aid, a library and documentation centre, and community awareness campaigns.

Counselling is the cornerstone of all Anweshi's services. The centre functions with two counsellors and one assistant counsellor, who are the first contact persons for the women who approach them. The counselling aims to provide women a safe and comfortable environment in which to discuss their problems and get advice on further action. The action proposed could be negotiation between the two parties or reconciliation through repeated counselling sessions, the filing of legal cases, or shelter at the short-stay home until a permanent solution is found. Community workers note the survivor's story and approach the accused perpetrator to encourage them to come to Anweshi to explain their side. The counselling can range from five to ten sessions, sometimes more. Anweshi respects and supports the decisions taken by survivors. In case the perpetrator refuses to cooperate, Anweshi's legal cell is consulted. The counsellors, community volunteers, and legal and paralegal staff coordinate their efforts.

Between 2011 and 2014, Anweshi's counselling centre handled about 1,000 new cases and 1,362 follow-up cases. Of these, 280 survivors are now living in environments free of violence.

Legal aid cell

Two advocates and one paralegal staffer manage the legal aid cell. They help in drafting petitions and registering cases at police stations (community workers usually visit the police station if the survivor decides to file a case against the perpetrator). They prepare agreement documents when the couple decides to reconcile and, in cases where no reconciliation is possible, they provide women free legal advice. One of the important functions of the legal cell is legal literacy classes for women in rural and urban areas. Between 2011 and 2014, Anweshi provided legal aid to 346 women and conducted about 100 legal literacy classes attended by 3,214 women. These classes cover gender dimensions and constitutional/legal rights as well as the protection and services available by law to women subjected to violence. The classes are conducted through anganwadis, mahila samajams (women's groups), women's self-help groups, and local NGOs.

Community awareness campaigns

Anweshi conducts community education and awareness programmes aimed at shattering the myth that violence against women is a private issue. Women are encouraged to disclose violence to their relatives and friends. The community work forms the link between the organisation, its target group, and the community. Anweshi trains women on sexuality, gender, and human rights; laws related to VAW; and practical advice, such as keeping certificates and documents safe in case they are forced out of the house. The campaigns aim to equip women who suffer violence with adequate knowledge and enable them to access services whenever they need them. Community workers are responsible for arranging these trainings, networking with anganwadi workers, Kudumbasree (a Kerala state initiative) members, mahila samajams, and other women's organisations in the district. As part of the awareness campaigns, community workers conducted 1,691 field visits between 2011 and 2014.

Anweshi also runs advocacy campaigns and workshops for implementing authorities such as the police and advocates to sensitise them about gender rights, discrimination, and gender-based violence.

Short-stay home

Between 2008 and 2014, Anweshi expanded its services to include a short-stay home, or temporary shelter, for women facing violence and their children. The shelter can accommodate at least 25 women and children. A psychologist visits the shelter regularly.

One of the cases referred to the short-stay home by the hospital and police was of a woman accused of killing her three children. She was referred there, as she was found to be mentally unstable. Anweshi's work with the woman revealed that she was, in fact, a victim of domestic violence. Her husband would assault her brutally in front of their children. In one despairing moment, she poisoned her children and tried to end her own life. She did not die, but she lost her children. She had been unable to deal with the shock of it until she came to Anweshi. Counselling and support enabled her to disclose the severity of the violence she faced, and with support from Anweshi, she has completed her graduation, remarried, and been reconciled with her parents.

Engaging adolescent girls through awareness programmes

Anweshi's experience has revealed that, besides women, adolescent girls are also at risk of rape, trafficking, molestation, and abuse. Awareness sessions for girls can help them make life-changing decisions. From 2006 onwards, Anweshi has been conducting age-appropriate classes and camps for adolescent boys and girls (and their parents, especially mothers), in schools and anganwadi centres, on gender rights and equality, violence, sexuality, sexual health, and physical and mental well-being. These classes also help identify children who face any kind of violence because they ask questions about their problem in class or approach the trainers directly or via telephone after class. From 2011 to 2014, Anweshi conducted six seminars, two workshops, and 120 classes attended by more than 2,500 participants. In 2012–13 alone, they counselled 44 students identified as facing violence. Another positive outcome of this project has been the Government of Kerala's notification that each school must appoint a counsellor.

Sound Alert is another of Anweshi's community projects in Kozhikode district. It creates mass awareness amongst women about gender-based violence and crisis intervention, setting up resource groups from amongst Kudumbasree workers, ASHA workers, and the social welfare department.

Alongside these awareness programmes, in 2010 Anweshi started publishing *Sanghaditha*, a platform for women from all walks of life to discuss gender and violence and bring these issues into the public domain. The magazine has an all-women editorial board.

Engagement with the health system

Any form of violence compromises the health and well-being of a woman. Violence involving perpetrators who are addicted to alcohol/drugs further complicates women's lives. A woman needs physical and psychological support to face the situation. However, most women do not disclose the violence to anybody even if there are serious physical injuries. Those who seek medical care report the cause of injuries as falls or accidents. Health professionals also tend to neglect or ignore such cases, sometimes because they lack the training to correctly identify the gender violence (especially domestic violence) but most often because they want to avoid the complications of a medico-legal case.

In this context, Anweshi recognised the need to extend its work to the health sector. It started the Anweshi Centre for Prevention of Gender-based Violence and Protection of Women's Health Rights (Actions through Health, Social, and Legal Interventions) project in July 2011.

The core objectives of the engagement with the health system are:

- To identify and support women survivors of violence coming for treatment to the Medical College Hospital (MCH), Kozhikode
- To sensitise health professionals at the hospital about violence against women as a public health issue
- To help all stakeholders develop the capacity and services to tackle gender-based violence at the grassroots

As a first step, a systematic cross-sectional survey was conducted among doctors, nurses, and other healthcare workers at MCH Kozhikode to understand their awareness and attitudes towards gender-based violence. Of the 288 health providers surveyed, 82.1% reported that they had not received any training on gender and women's health, and about 92% had not received any training on VAW. Most of them reported lack of infrastructure and expertise in this domain as a major obstacle to dealing with the health consequences of gender-based violence.

Anweshi envisaged a health system approach based on CEHAT's Dilaasa model and planned for a healthcare and crisis centre for women in partnership with MCH Kozhikode. The first contact persons would be doctors or nurses, who would be responsible for identifying women experiencing violence and providing treatment. They would then refer survivors for counselling at the care centre and other forms of support as required.

Key components of the model

Healthcare and crisis management centre

Despite Anweshi's efforts to engage with the administrators of the hospital, however, the crisis centre within MCH Kozhikode did not materialise. In 2011, the Anweshi healthcare centre was set up close to MCH, and it worked to sensitise health professionals. However, the initiative was not successful because the hospital, overburdened with cases from all the northern districts of Kerala, did not identify or refer any women. Although many survivors of violence invariably contact the health system, they do not get the attention they deserve from hospitals.

Nevertheless, Anweshi continued to engage with the hospital through ward rounds, speaking to female patients. It also offered crisis intervention services to women identified as survivors of domestic violence. Anweshi has official permission to check the casualty register to identify cases of gender-based violence. It ensures adequate treatment and follow-up, with counselling and legal aid in accordance with the woman's preference.

Capacity-building

Capacity-building to equip health providers to respond to VAW was a major objective of the project. Anweshi conducted training sessions for health professionals, including doctors, nurses, and nursing students, on how to identify violence cases correctly, the legal prospects of such cases, the PWDV Act, the role and response of healthcare providers, and referral to the Anweshi crisis centre. Most of the doctors and nurses consented to the process and attended training sessions. In addition, Anweshi conducted sensitisation programmes for medical officers from primary health centres (PHCs) in Kozhikode, gender-based violence management (GBVM) coordinators, and ASHA workers under the National Health Mission to enable them to identify and refer cases to Anweshi and provide medical support. Between 2011 and 2014, Anweshi conducted four workshops and 14 seminars for 312 participants, including doctors, nurses, and medical and nursing students. Anweshi continues to conduct such training sessions for health providers from different parts of the district on request.

Referral system

Anweshi has a good referral system in place, one that includes the police, health professionals, protection officers, GBVM coordinators, community workers, and legal staff. Women approach Anweshi through them as well as through the legal literacy classes and awareness campaigns. However, most often, friends, neighbours, or relatives refer women to Anweshi. Of 102 referrals in 2013–14, 74 were referred by friends or relatives. Establishing a referral system specifically targeting unreported cases of violence coming to the medical college hospital was important, as female patients admitted to the hospital with burns are most often victims of domestic violence. They usually hide the truth, believing they have no choice but to hide the violence. The result is that the perpetrators get away even if the victim loses her life.

Referral is a two-way process. Anweshi also refers patients to hospitals, psychiatrists, police, rehabilitation centres, de-addiction centres, and so on. In 2013–14, Anweshi referred seven cases to the police, seven to psychiatrists, and three to de-addiction centres.

Advocacy for a health system approach

Representatives of Anweshi conducted a multi-level campaign and had discussions with the state health minister to convey the need for a health system approach for effective implementation of the VAW project. Anweshi's advocacy influences policymakers, albeit indirectly. Bhoomika, a Kerala government initiative to tackle GBV, is evidence of this. Bhoomika functions in all district hospitals of Kerala, providing medical care and treatment to survivors. It refers clients to Anweshi for legal aid. In addition, Anweshi trains GBVM coordinators at Bhoomika centres. There is an active collaboration with the National Health Mission (NHM), Kozhikode. NHM invites representatives from Anweshi to its meetings, refers cases that are beyond the capacity of Bhoomika, and supports Anweshi's endeavours.

Outreach with the health system

Anweshi always advocates for grassroots decision-making and tries to ensure that survivors make informed decisions. As part of its engagement with the health system, Anweshi strengthened its outreach activities and started classes and seminars for PHC medical officers, nurses, ASHA workers, and other community volunteers. The aim was to develop resources and services at the grassroots and ensure that women are provided the necessary knowledge to access such services. Eight seminars for lawyers, journalists, police officials, writers, homemakers, ASHA, and anganwadi workers have been conducted.

Maintaining an active network of communication

Anweshi collaborates with like-minded organisations all over the country and maintains an active network of knowledge-sharing. It also collaborates with the state government's Bhoomika initiative. Anweshi works in partnership with organisations such as Sahayathrika, a transgender organisation; Sakhi (Thiruvananthapuram); and CEHAT. Anweshi is also part of the Safe City: Free of Violence against Women and Girls Initiative, conducted by Sakhi Women's Resource Centre with the support of the United Nations Development Fund for Women (UNIFEM) and Jagori, Delhi.

Reflections and challenges

After almost four years of collaboration with the health sector, Anweshi has had many achievements – and some failures. The sensitisation and community awareness programmes have met their objectives, with an increasing number of new cases being referred to Anweshi. The number of new cases through health sector interventions almost doubled between 2012 (31) and 2014 (56). Consultation services increased fourfold, from 24 to 98, during the same period. The number of women and children admitted in the short-stay home also increased from 31 to 66 and 18 to 33 respectively. In addition, Anweshi has been given the responsibility of managing the Nirbhaya Centre in Kozhikode district, which is evidence of the credibility the organisation has acquired over the years. The referrals from MCH Kozhikode indicate that there is a clear need for such services for survivors of violence.

At the same time, the success of the Anweshi healthcare centre has fallen somewhat short of expectations. The number of referrals from MCH hospital was 27 in 2012 but fell to seven in 2014, pointing to declining interest from health professionals in identifying cases of violence. This could be because of their heavy workload or because there is a continued reluctance to accept their responsibility to survivors of violence. However, Anweshi is still trying to set up the crisis centre within the hospital.

No follow-up of cases is done after a reconciliation, but several women do come back to Anweshi following repeated episodes of violence. Even though Anweshi covers the northern districts of Kerala, health interventions are limited to Kozhikode. These are the major limitations of Anweshi's engagement with the health sector.

That Anweshi's engagement with the social welfare department and Bhoomika and its advocacy are reaching policymakers is evident from the fact that it has been assigned responsibility for the Nirbhaya Centre. Still, Anweshi's confrontationist image among politicians and bureaucrats does hamper active involvement at the policy level. Anweshi works on its own agenda and does not allow political influences to alter its strategy. Moreover, Anweshi has been instrumental in exposing some controversial cases with long-term political consequences. One such was the "ice cream parlour abuse case" ten years ago, involving a former minister. Anweshi took up the issue of forced prostitution of young girls by prominent politicians and approached the court. Following this, there have been many misconceptions about Anweshi's work, but this is also changing.

The most important impact of the programme, however, has been that women from both rural and urban areas recognise Anweshi as their hope and shelter. In a health setting, women can access medical care and services without fear or stigma. This enhances their confidence. If healthcare providers actively identify signs and symptoms of violence, no case of violence will go unreported. Eventually, the incidence of violence against women may be substantially reduced. However, this calls for a change in the mindset of healthcare providers, including women. Sensitisation programmes may not result in a complete change of attitude, but such a change is necessary to develop adequate facilities and personnel to deal with GBV. The social and personal stigma the survivor has to face also needs to be addressed.

Consistent efforts with the health system, as with any other system, require resources. This has proved to be a major challenge. Health interventions call for strong political will, and sustainability of the programmes depends on availability of funds.

Anweshi's future efforts will focus on starting the crisis management centre *within* the health system, establishing a long-term rehabilitation facility and follow-up even after reconciliation or settlement and continuing sensitisation programmes and outreach activities. Anweshi does not have a plan to expand its services to the entire state, as this is beyond its capability at present.

Anweshi already functions as a one-stop crisis centre (OSCC), its activities going hand in hand with those envisaged for the government's OSCC schemes and Nirbhaya Centres.

Anweshi was born of the women's movement, with a focus on ensuring the basic human rights of women. Over the years, it has evolved to an understanding that physical and mental health and well-being are an integral part of the human rights of women.

Section 4

Working with health workers in rural and semi-urban areas

Introduction

This section presents two models set up to address violence and respond to the healthcare needs of women and girls in a rural context.

The Mahila Sarvangeen Utkarsh Mandal (MASUM) case study describes efforts made in remote pockets of rural Maharashtra to provide health services to women from the oppressed castes and minority religion. Established as a feminist rural organisation, MASUM observed that doctors in the rural health delivery system were not very regular and that the shortage of women doctors deters women from seeking services, especially reproductive health services. Women did not discuss health conditions such as white discharge, tuberculosis, and urinary incontinence for fear of stigma and desertion. Most rural women would end up working in the fields of rich farmers and would often face sexual violence, but there was no way to get these issues addressed.

MASUM recognised the multiple levels of deprivation these women suffered and decided to work with women from the community to enable them to stop violence and take charge of their own health. The MASUM case study presents two important initiatives: the Sadafuli Centres for women's health concerns and the Sathi Centres to address violence faced by women. These models recognise that women from marginalised castes and classes may not be able to access health services, and therefore women from within these castes and classes need to be trained to guide others in their community. The two centres interface with each other, as it is a well-established fact that ill health causes violence and violence leads to poor health.

The MASUM case study is a unique example of how rural community women can be mobilised to deal with violence themselves. It describes strategies such as involving village elders and using nonviolent techniques to confront abusers.

The Rural Women's Social Education Centre (RUWSEC), a grassroots women's organisation, was set up in 1981 in 12 villages of (erstwhile) Chengalpattu taluka near Chennai in Tamil Nadu. Besides T K Sundari Ravindran, a founder of the organisation, the other founding members were 12 Dalit women whose experience and knowledge of the day-to-day struggles and oppression of marginalised women prompted them to come together to form RUWSEC. The organisation aimed to achieve gender equality and enable access to sexual and reproductive health and rights. These goals were to be realised through the participation of women (and men) – especially Dalits – and the promotion of leadership skills to influence existing governance and accountability structures and foster critical thinking and alternative models in healthcare provisioning, research, and planning for social action.

RUWSEC soon realised that the formal public health system was inadequate, and it therefore decided to put pressure on it. At the same time, women facing violence also had healthcare needs and required different kinds of interventions. This case study demonstrates the ways in which men and women from the community were equipped to deal with violence. There is a well laid out system for training local men and women to provide care and support to women and, when required, to refer them to the RUWSEC clinic for additional medical aid, psychological support, and police and legal aid. The case study highlights ways in which communities can themselves mitigate violence and create an environment of zero tolerance of any form of violence against women.

Both MASUM and RUWSEC are rural women's collectives, organising women from marginalised communities in particular. Their focus has been on empowering women and raising issues of caste discrimination and gender at the village level. VAW is one of the many issues they have worked on with local leadership and panchayats. They have responded to individual survivors and developed an ecosystem at the community level that supports survivors and questions the violent behaviour of men against women. They have set up mechanisms at the local level to provide immediate support to survivors and worked with PHCs and rural hospitals to create awareness about these services so that health providers can refer women to them. RUWSEC has even endeavoured to provide counselling services at the PHC.

Both are good examples of how communities can be engaged in responding to individual women's experiences of violence and how zero tolerance of domestic violence environments can be built at the community level by engaging various stakeholders. These are examples that the health system can learn from when designing interventions on VAW at the primary level, keeping the sociopolitical context of rural communities in mind.

4.1 MASUM

Ramesh Awasthi

MASUM trains women in rural Maharashtra to take charge of their health and break the cycle of gender-based violence and ill health.

Introduction

Mahila Sarvangeen Utkarsh Mandal (MASUM) was set up in 1987 as a community-based women's organisation working in Maharashtra (Pune and Ahmednagar districts). While there are some industrial pockets and well-developed urban centres in these districts of western Maharashtra, the rural areas are mainly agricultural. Purandar (Pune district) and Parner (Ahmednagar district) are perennially drought-prone, with very little assured irrigation. The women of drought-prone villages in Purandar taluka were organised to address the issues that affect their lives. Most of them were from oppressed castes and minority religions. Those belonging to the middle class suffered violence at home or had left their husbands but lacked the support of the natal family. Many of them worked for daily wages in the fields of rich farmers, often facing economic exploitation and sexual abuse. The women thus faced structural violence as well as physical/sexual violence from their families. They came together to support each other and collectively fight for their rights. MASUM gradually evolved as a development group with a feminist perspective and democratic approach.

Women experiencing physical, emotional, and sexual violence suffer grave and enduring physical and mental health consequences. Survivors suffer injuries, burns (often fatal), sexually transmitted diseases, unwanted pregnancies, sexual dysfunction, chronic muscular cramps and pain, anxiety, headaches, hyper-acidity, depression, chronic fatigue, sleep and eating disorders, suicidal ideation and attempts, and persistent feelings of rejection and vulnerability, contributing to high morbidity and mortality, especially in the reproductive age group (WHO 2010). In addition, women who left violent homes or were forced to leave home by the perpetrator were left homeless, as they rarely received the support of the natal family. The natal family often pushed the daughter back into the violent marital home to be rid of the burden and stigma of a married daughter living with her parents. Brothers, too, wanted a married sister off their hands irrespective of the likely consequences to her body and mind lest they had to part with some of the inherited property, never mind that she had a legal right to it.

The links between violence and health were also manifest in women's lives. Women with tuberculosis, mental illness, or HIV/AIDS were deprived of the necessary healthcare; suffered stigma, neglect, and isolation; and were often sent off to the natal family. Therefore, many women were reluctant to get their illnesses diagnosed and properly treated (WHO 2005). Women were more vulnerable to ill health because of their low status in society, poor access to food, and excessive workload at home and in the fields. When a woman did go to a health centre – public or private – she would not speak of the violence in her life because of the family "honour" and the likely repercussions, such as increased violence, further restrictions on mobility, or being driven out of the home. A woman caught in such a cycle of violence and ill health needs help to get healthcare, counselling, and legal assistance to break out of it and live a life of dignity.

Addressing health issues

The health systems (public or private) did not address the specific health-care needs of these rural women, especially those facing violence at home, and no government or private agency provided them counselling and legal assistance. MASUM pivoted its interventions on the creation of a cadre of community-based workers to address women's health issues and violence against women. This local resource of trained and motivated women would take up these issues at the community level as well as with government systems. The initial training of health and paralegal workers was conducted with different sets of people, and the two programmes were launched more or less simultaneously. The village-based health centres called Sadafuli Centres (meaning "a flower that blooms all through the year") and first-contact counselling centres called Sathi Centres (meaning "comrade" or "friend") were located at premises provided by the village council (panchayat). They were inaugurated at public functions by the council chairperson to build community acceptance and ownership of the programmes.

The health workers were local women, particularly those from the oppressed/marginalised communities, and single women – the point being that when rich, upper caste women came to them for help, the power equations would begin to change. The selected women were trained for two years, with periodic refresher trainings thereafter. The women came for three-day residential training workshops once a month over two years. Following each training workshop, the women went back to their villages and conducted with women in different communities group meetings at which they talked about their health issues, local practices of dealing with those issues, and what they had learned. These group meetings served the dual purpose of learning from members of the community and establishing a rapport with them.

The training included building a feminist perspective about a woman's body and health as well as sharing knowledge of various health issues, management of common ailments, use of local herbs, and the use, dosage, and side effects of allopathic medicines for common ailments. The health workers were trained to take medical history and blood pressure, test haemoglobin, and conduct breast examinations.

They also acquired the skills to do bimanual and speculum examinations to identify uterine prolapse, take Pap smears, and perform VIA (visual inspection with acetic acid) screenings for detection of cervical cancer. They in turn taught village women about the management and treatment of common ailments, including reproductive tract infections (RTIs) and uterine prolapse, providing herbal and allopathic medicines at very low cost, preparing herbal vaginal pessaries, and doing pelvic exercises to prevent worsening of a prolapsed uterus. The health workers were trained to develop a broader understanding of the social, cultural, and political context, with a gender perspective and human rights–based approach. The trainings were closed-door sessions. Within a couple of days, the process of seeing each other's bodies, looking at one's own body, and practising speculum examinations on each other cultivated increased levels of interpersonal confidence and intimacy amongst the participants. This process was initiated with two resource persons demonstrating speculum examinations on each other. With the initial resistance disappearing, the women discussed their own reproductive and sexual health issues freely in the group.

The health workers addressed the health issues of women who came to the Sadafuli Centres and those who attended special detection camps. They treated menstrual disorders, white and red vaginal discharge, uterine prolapse, general weakness, anaemia and backache, joint pain, and so on. For serious and chronic ailments, the Sadafulis explained the problem to women and referred them to public health services.

Addressing violence against women

The two-year training of local women selected to address VAW followed the same strategy used to train Sadafulis: three-day residential training workshops every month, followed by community meetings in their own village. The training involved understanding gender; patriarchy; gender-based discrimination; gender-based violence; the intersectionality of gender and caste, class, illness, age, physical ability, and sexual orientation; the cycle of violence; violence in natal homes; feminist counselling; women-related laws; and suicide prevention.

These village-based paralegal workers functioned as first-contact counsellors. They helped survivors of violence in safety planning, arranging safe homes in the village for the woman in crisis, helping the woman get in touch with her natal family or any friend she felt safe with, helping her file a police report or legal case if she wished to, and referring her to

MASUM's counselling centre in the taluka town for counselling and legal help. These first-contact counsellors were also trained in suicide prevention counselling, and they helped women with suicidal ideation, dissuading them from attempting suicide or inflicting self-harm. An example of first contact counsellors responding to survivors of violence is presented in Box 4.1.1.

Box 4.1.1 Example of Sathi centres providing support to VAW survivors

Sujata, a support group woman from a village near Saswad, had noticed that Manda, a 25-year-old woman living in her lane, had been looking a bit low, not talking much to anyone. One day she saw Manda walking towards a well without any vessel or load of clothes. She observed distress in Manda's walk and body movements. Sujata left all her work, rushed after Manda, and talked to her directly about her suicidal ideation.

After a few minutes of conversation and a little persuasion, Sujata managed to take Manda to her own house. Sujata offered her some tea, explained that suicide would not solve her problems, and counselled her to seek help from the Sathi Centre in the village or the counselling centre at Saswad rather than ending her life or harming herself. She accompanied Manda to the Sathi Centre, where trained paralegal counsellors discussed her options and prepared a safety plan with her. Support group members living near Manda's house talked to her regularly as a follow-up safety measure.

MASUM set up a counselling centre in Saswad, the taluka town, with full-time trained counsellors and a lawyer who visited twice a week for legal advice. The taluka town is well connected to most villages by road and is a marketplace, too, so women from all over the taluka can visit the counselling centre on the pretext of going to the weekly market. Over the years, the centre has helped more than 3,000 women with issues such as violence and harassment by the husband and his family, second marriage by the husband, maintenance of the woman and her children, custody of children, retrieval of streedhan (her valuables) from the husband's house after separation, right to parental property, obtaining a separate ration card for single women, protection under the PWDV Act, and the filing of police complaints.

The paralegal workers mobilise village communities to oppose VAW and promote women's right to a life free of violence and discrimination. They organise local support groups of both women and willing gender-sensitive men to intervene in episodes of violence against women. They support survivors in speaking up and intervene with the family as well as the village council or local dispute resolution committee for justice for the woman survivor. Box 4.1.2 provides an example of the functioning of support groups in the community.

Strongly rooted in a patriarchal culture, the men of the village supported MASUM's interventions when it helped a daughter from the village, but when it came to daughters-in-law, the entire kinship disapproved of MASUM's actions. However, in one case, a MASUM staffer, who is herself a local daughter-in-law, managed to mobilise other women and some sensitive men against violence. Such cases and dialogues are part of the ongoing process of change.

MASUM believes that societal acceptance of a woman's course of action is necessary if she is to live with reasonable dignity and have a violence-free and rightful place in the family and community. While legislation guaranteeing justice for the woman makes a lot of difference in her empowerment, we still need to engage with the community so that community structures change to recognise every woman's basic human right to live in an atmosphere free of violence and discrimination (Awasthi 2013).

Box 4.1.2 Snapshot of support centre functions by MASUM

Kusum, a 32-year-old widow, lived with her five-year-old daughter in a small village near Saswad. When women from the support group heard that a man from another village had assaulted Kusum with a sharp weapon, they rushed to her house and helped her dress the wound. Fortunately, she escaped the assault with a minor cut. The support group women soon found that the village men (including the village leaders) were not in favour of helping this woman since, though a widow, she was having sexual relations with a married man from another village and hence was a "bad woman" who was better thrown out of the village. However, the support group talked to Kusum in detail and found that the man who assaulted her had been hitting her and threatening her with murder unless she went to live with him in a third village. Not being sure of this man, Kusum did not want to leave the village.

The support group supported her right to enter into and walk out of the relationship and helped her file a police complaint with guidance from MASUM's counselling centre at Saswad. The man did not dare visit her again, and because of MASUM's intervention, the village leadership could not take any action against the woman.

Links between the two centres

Cross-referrals between the health centre and counselling centre have been quite common. Some women found it easier to come to the health centre with the excuse of getting a tablet for a headache but actually just wanting to lie down quietly, unwind, and talk about the episode of violence at home. Some with an injury or pain (reporting the injury as caused by a bullock or blunt object) would come for a dressing or painkiller but open up after a while and recount the violence when probed. These women were encouraged to go to MASUM's counselling centre, speak up, and seek help. Women were generally very reluctant to speak about sexual violence, but when they came for a speculum examination for RTI complaints, they would share their experience of sexual violence, which was sometimes very severe and bizarre.

Counsellors at the counselling centres have received training in recording forensic evidence of injuries – descriptive as well as photographic. Before referring a survivor of violence to the healthcare centre, counsellors record forensic documentation to challenge, if needed, manipulation of the medical certificate at the level of the health centre. In spite of violence involving physical injuries, women do not want to file a medico-legal case since most of them prefer a settlement, with the man signing an agreement not to resort to violence so that she can live with her husband peacefully.

To reach out to more and more women, MASUM regularly conducts training sessions on VAW with the Integrated Child Development Service (ICDS) and ASHA workers in Purandar and Daund blocks. ICDS and ASHA workers are regularly in touch with young pregnant women and young mothers. Sensitised to VAW, these workers can identify women suffering violence and encourage them to seek help. Following these sessions, ICDS workers have been referring women suffering violence to MASUM's counselling centres. ICDS workers themselves have also accessed help at the counselling centre.

MASUM has advised doctors and paramedics at the rural hospital (RH) located in the same taluka town to refer their patients who have survived violence to MASUM for counselling, and these referrals are being made.

Approaches to working on health issues with women from the community

1   Women in villages have very poor access to healthcare for multiple reasons: low status in the family, poor self-image, no decision-making power, restricted mobility, body shame combined with scarcity of women doctors in rural areas, and dysfunctional public health services. MASUM believed that doctor-dependent healthcare services would not increase access of the rural poor, especially women, and their primary healthcare needs could best be served by community-based, properly trained paramedics (women from the community) duly supported by referral services for secondary and tertiary care.

2 MASUM's health programme has been designed to focus on women's health issues with a rights-based approach and on feminist principles – empowering, woman-controlled – with interventions devoid of hierarchy between healthcare provider and recipient. Women are taught self-examination of breasts, and the speculum examination is done in a reclining position such that a woman can see her body in a mirror. Self-help is empowering for women. MASUM encourages women to use public health services at the village, block, and district level, and all women suspected of having precancerous changes of the cervix (on VIA screening) are referred to the district hospital for further treatment.

3 MASUM does not purport to assume the role of a women's health service provider. MASUM's experience has established that low-cost, high-quality services for early detection of cervical cancer as well as detection and management of other gynaecological morbidities can be provided by well-trained community-level women health workers. Convinced by MASUM's approach, the Government of Maharashtra's Department of Non-Communicable Diseases (NCD) invited MASUM to train their ANMs, lady health visitors (LHVs), and medical officers in one block of Satara district and 13 blocks of Pune district in VIA screening techniques.

Challenges

1 Social barriers prevent women from reporting violence and accessing healthcare. Women's access to healthcare is restricted by shame of the body, patriarchal notions, low self-image, and a heavy burden of work and chores. Health workers often have to negotiate with the husband and parents-in-law to arrange for the woman to go to the health centre. The pressure of preserving the family honour and the belief that what happens between husband and wife should not be discussed beyond the four walls of the house prevent them from reporting or seeking help. Reporting sexual violence becomes even rarer.

2 Addressing the structural violence that causes health problems in women is an arduous task. The common cause of prolapsed uterus in agricultural communities is the very short (barely one week) resting period allowed to women after delivering a baby. Women are considered "free labour" in the family, and farmer households (in-laws) try to minimise the resting period.

3 The greedy invasion of women's bodies by the private healthcare sector is rampant in India. Doctors in the private sector vie with each other to carry out hysterectomies on women with minor menstrual problems; it is like, "who gets her first"? Women in the 25–35 age group who are forced into menopause suffer consequences such as osteoporosis and early onset of ageing. MASUM's efforts to identify cervical cancer and other gynaecological morbidities assume significance in this scenario.

4   The poor state of public health services and the near absence of mental health services in rural areas leave women little choice but to endure ill health or give in to the unregulated and exploitative private health sector.
5   Women do speak up about sexual violence once they develop a rapport with the counsellor, and women in all age groups face sexual violence. Counselling of male partners is also necessary to address this issue.

Major lessons

1   Empowering feminist counselling helps a survivor overcome low self-image, look after her health, and negotiate for her rights from an empowered position.
2   Women suffering violence need simultaneous access to healthcare and counselling.
3   MASUM's multiple development intervention programmes in the community help MASUM staff reach out to a large number of women in villages, and the inter-linkages among programmes enable the staff to identify and help women in crisis get healthcare and address violence. Multifaceted interventions also blunt the community backlash.
4   Women's empowerment is essential but not sufficient to address the barriers to women's access to healthcare and the structural violence caused by patriarchal norms. The participation of men, young people, and children is also needed to challenge gender norms and promote a culture of gender equality. MASUM works with men, young people (14–25 years), and children (8–14 years) towards this goal. The results have been encouraging.

References

Awasthi, R (2013): "Negotiating with community-based groups and structures from a feminist perspective," in *Feminist counselling and domestic violence in India*, P Bhate-Deosthali, S Rege and P Prakash (eds.), New Delhi, India: Routledge, pp. 256–276.
WHO (2005): *WHO multi-country study on women's health and domestic violence against women*, Geneva: World Health Organization.
WHO (2010): *Preventing intimate partner and sexual violence against women: Taking action and generating evidence*, Geneva: World Health Organization and London School of Hygiene and Tropical Medicine.

4.2 Rural Women's Social Education Centre (RUWSEC)

P Balasubramanian, Bhuvaneswari Sunil, and T K Sundari Ravindran

Dalit women in rural Tamil Nadu learn to voice and prevent gender-based violence.

Introduction

In the early 1980s, in Vallam village near Chennai, Tamil Nadu, a group of Dalit women began to meet and question their oppression for the very first time. The meetings were part of the National Adult Education Programme and were facilitated by gender and health activist T K Sundari Ravindran. The meetings also gave women the opportunity to discuss their reproductive health concerns. Their own experiences and realisation of the day-to-day struggles and oppression of other marginalised women prompted 12 Dalit women, along with Sundari Ravindran, to form the Rural Women's Social Education Centre (RUWSEC) in 1981. The premise for this grassroots women's collective was that, in a patriarchal society, women's lack of control over their bodies and lives leads to the further marginalisation of women, negatively impacting their reproductive health and well-being.

RUWSEC's mission since inception has been to ensure the well-being of women from poor and marginalised communities and to empower them to stand up for their rights and act as agents of social change. Gender equality and sexual and reproductive health and rights (SRHR) have been their goals. RUWSEC's approach is to amplify the voices of women (and men), especially Dalits; to promote leadership skills so that communities can participate effectively in existing governance and accountability structures; and to foster critical thinking and alternative models in healthcare provision, research, and planning for social action.

Prevention of violence against women programme

Since the early 1980s, RUWSEC has been providing legal, psychosocial, and economic support to village women, including some RUWSEC staffers who have experienced spousal violence. RUWSEC's interventions remained reactive and ad hoc until the tragic death of a RUWSEC community worker, who was set aflame by her husband. That was the turning point. When the community, including many women leaders, helped the woman's husband hide from the police, RUWSEC members realised that something was very wrong. The community-based women's organisation was taking on all the responsibility of challenging spousal violence while the community often actively aided the perpetrator or, at best, did nothing to stop him. They saw clearly the need to make the community responsible for stopping spousal violence against women (Balasubramanian and Ravindran 2010). A household survey conducted by RUWSEC in 1997 showed that 25% of the women experienced domestic violence, predominantly physical and emotional violence, including sexual violence. The violence caused physical injuries, repeated unwanted pregnancies, and abortions, which arose due to non-consensual sex (RUWSEC 1998–99).

In 1998, the Prevention of Violence Against Women (PoVAW) programme was introduced as a sustainable, rights-oriented, gender-sensitive, and community-based collective intervention on SRHR, with a proactive and systemic approach. The broad objective of the programme is to (i) get domestic violence acknowledged as a major gender justice and health problem among key actors in the local community, policymakers, and service providers and (ii) to create support services for affected women, providing legal and medical support, information, and skills that will help them deal with the problem.

Figure 4.2.1 depicts the three main components of the PoVAW programme, and the subsequent text provides further details.

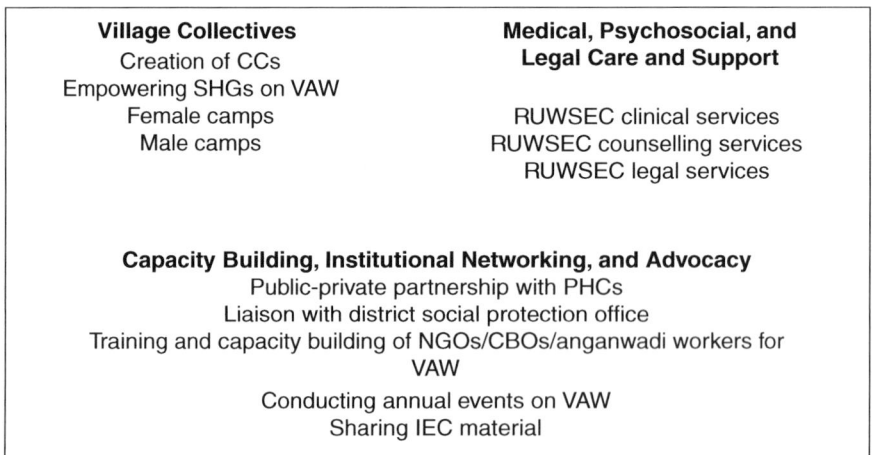

Village Collectives Creation of CCs Empowering SHGs on VAW Female camps Male camps	**Medical, Psychosocial, and Legal Care and Support** RUWSEC clinical services RUWSEC counselling services RUWSEC legal services

Capacity Building, Institutional Networking, and Advocacy
Public-private partnership with PHCs
Liaison with district social protection office
Training and capacity building of NGOs/CBOs/anganwadi workers for VAW
Conducting annual events on VAW
Sharing IEC material

Figure 4.2.1 Key components of the PoVAW programme by RUWSEC
Source: Compiled by authors.

Community-based committees

The core component of the PoVAW programme is the establishment of community-based committees (CCs) at the village level. Initially set up in five villages on a pilot basis in 1998, the committees were launched in 90 backward villages across four administrative blocks in the district. Constraints of funding and other factors have since narrowed down the intervention to 25 villages in one block. The CCs intervene to resolve VAW at the local level and act as pressure groups, sustaining advocacy at the local level. Each CC is carefully constituted, with five to six members, including at least two or three women whose husbands support their involvement. The rest of the members are influential women representatives from self-help groups, youth volunteers, or elected panchayat members. Men who play an active role in RUWSEC's gender-sensitisation programmes and who are known not to abuse their wives or be addicted to alcohol are also included. The local people call the CCs "women's protection committees," and the members function as volunteers without any financial compensation. The strategy has yielded good outcomes and positive feedback from the community and committee members. The process of training CC members is dealt with in the sub-section on capacity-building later.

Support services to women affected by gender-based violence

The case histories of women in this block suggest that sexual violence and dowry issues are major causes of the violence women experience. The irresponsibility, alcoholism, and extra-marital relationships of husbands also frame the context for VAW. RUWSEC offered centralised counselling services on broader health issues, including GBV, at five PHCs but currently offers them at only one PHC in the RUWSEC block. Each CC handles six to ten cases annually and refers two or three cases to RUWSEC's centralised team located in Karumarappakkam, which includes doctors and provides counselling and medical services in addition to referral for legal aid and livelihood-related services. Between 2012 and 2018, 257 women in Thirukazhukundrum block accessed the centralised counselling and medical services. Eight unmarried girls also accessed counselling and medical abortion services. Eleven women with mental health problems were given first-level psychosocial counselling and then referred to The Banyan, which provides specialised mental healthcare services in Tamil Nadu. RUWSEC also counselled 172 spouses at the women's request and with their consent (RUWSEC 2012–18).

Clara, a CC member since 2014, from Karumarapakkam village, says she has learnt a lot from RUWSEC's training. "I tolerated the violence of my first husband because I was not aware," she says. She became a member of the CC because she did not want any other woman or child to go through what she did. "Our CC has resolved the problems of 15 families," she says.

"Many women in the village come to talk to us because they know our work and trust us."

Capacity-building

The CCs undergo intensive training at a series of 18-day workshops over two years. The trainings consist of two main modules: (i) introducing violence as a gender, social justice, and health issue and establishing an appreciation of its many dimensions and complexities and (ii) developing leadership, problem-solving, and counselling skills on diverse themes. These themes include the social determinants of health, gender, and health equity; the legal dimensions of domestic violence and sexual harassment at the workplace; the reproductive health consequences of domestic violence; and resolving issues of violence at the level of the child, adolescent, and adult. The pedagogy of the training includes deliberations, role-play, skits, case history analysis, and group games. This participatory learning approach enables both men and women to learn how to bring about gender-related changes in attitude and behaviour. Besides training to resolve issues at the individual/family level, the CCs are also trained to refer women to shelter homes and file a complaint at a police station with support from the district social protection officer and the RUWSEC advocate. They attend court proceedings and offer emotional and financial support to the petitioners. Experienced CC members take refresher courses once a year to update themselves on these topics. These refresher courses also serve as a platform where committee members share their experiences from the field. Sixty-five CC members trained before 2012 go through refresher trainings once or twice a year.

In the absence of regular contact, however, some of the CCs in villages are no longer active. Only 50% to 60% of the old CCs are active at present.

In addition to forming and building the capacity of CCs, RUWSEC has worked to raise awareness of VAW amongst community leaders and young people. The intention is to create broad-based support in the community for PoVAW. Grassroots-level workers, such as anganwadi workers or ICDS and self-help group (SHG) members, who have a strong rapport with young and married women, are trained to identify and address issues of domestic violence at two- to four-day workshops in their villages.

Identifying and nurturing young leaders in the community so that they function as future promoters of gender equality and health is another key strategy. These young leaders attend gender-sensitisation workshops and meetings. RUWSEC gives one-day sessions on gender and GBV as part of school- and community-based life skills education for adolescents and young people. Over 700 adolescents and young people participate annually in this programme. Workshops on gender equality and workplace challenges for young women employed in companies across different sectors in the region enable women to support colleagues who are in vulnerable situations.

Men play an important role in the prevention of spousal violence. Awareness camps for men inform them of the consequences of domestic violence on the health of women and the legal provisions that protect women from violence. Special workshops every six months train married men below 45 years of age on GBV and reproductive health.

CC members and others attend candlelight marches and awareness meetings on International Women's Day (March 8) and during the 16-day (November 25 to December 10) international campaign against gender-based violence. These were initially conducted on a large scale, but in recent years these campaigns are being held at the village level.

Advocacy and institutional development

Mixed groups comprising survivors of violence and their parents, siblings, and relatives are invited for support group meetings every six months. These spaces encourage communities to discuss their issues and break the silence and social stigma around VAW. The meetings have gathered strength and become more meaningful with the incorporation of sessions on life skills, legal aid, and understanding violence. The presence of parents and siblings has given survivors of violence the courage to move away from their husbands and face society with confidence.

RUWSEC also strives to strengthen its institutional network at the meso and macro levels to sustain and upscale the PoVAW model. The larger aim is to influence policymakers and promote a culture of zero tolerance of gender violence at the governance level. These policymakers include health officials, district-level social protection officers, and police officials, all of whom are critical in the battle against VAW. Annual meetings with policymakers and officials address issues pertinent to the prevention of violence against women. Mutual understanding and professional partnership are developed and sustained with all of them. Some officials are invited to these meetings and awareness campaigns as speakers. This adds to their accountability.

Reflections and challenges

From an acceptance of violence as the destiny of a woman, women who have been empowered by RUWSEC are today able to decide and act independently on gender-based violence. RUWSEC has been successful in conscientising women on issues of violence and safeguarding them against violence. Women generally want to resolve issues locally through community support rather than resorting to legal measures or shelter homes, and most of the women trained believe they are now empowered to do so. Women have gained the confidence to enter a police station and file a complaint against their husbands without fear or hesitation. They do not shy away from demanding divorce either. They guide and support other women in similar circumstances.

However, several challenges remain. RUWSEC has been unable to extend its work to a larger number of villages because of a paucity of funds. Retaining trained and skilled CC members is also challenging in a patriarchal culture. Counselling and medical services are imperative in addressing VAW, but the lack of public health institutions to accommodate counsellors at all levels acts as a barrier in upscaling the programme. On the legal front, even after gender-sensitisation on issues surrounding violence against women, social protection officers and police officers tend to remain insensitive and unwilling to take action. There is a need to enhance the capacities of like-minded NGOs and other state and corporate actors as well.

Following several years of sustained and dedicated intervention and advocacy efforts, the ability of women to voice and prevent GBV is heartening. However, patriarchal attitudes and practices still need to change, as the surveys conducted by RUWSEC in 1997 and 2012 indicate.

References

Balasubramanian, P and Ravindran, S T K (2010): "Promoting zero tolerance for spousal violence: A community-based intervention in rural Tamil Nadu, India," Arrow for Change 11, Asian Pacific Resource and Research Centre for Women.

RUWSEC (1997): "Baseline survey reports 1997," (unpublished), Rural Women's Social Education Centre, Thirukazhukundrum, Tamil Nadu.

RUWSEC (1998–99; 2012–18): "Annual reports," Rural Women's Social Education Centre, Thirukazhukundrum, Tamil Nadu.

RUWSEC (2012): "Baseline survey reports 2012," (unpublished), Rural Women's Social Education Centre, Thirukazhukundrum, Tamil Nadu.

Section 5

Advocacy with the health sector

Introduction

This section describes the efforts of two organisations – Sama and Tathapi – to train health providers and advocate with the health system for the recognition of VAW as a public health issue.

Sama is a member of different health coalitions, including the People's Health Movement (PHM) and the Medico Friend Circle (MFC). It has consistently raised issues of women's health – coercive population policies, health rights of women in unorganised sectors such as mining, VAW and the ethics of reproductive technology – in its engagements with progressive movements. Sama has advocated with both the public and private health sector to recognise VAW as a health issue. This case study describes these efforts. Sama's research and advocacy agenda builds on evidence pertaining to the health consequences of violence, the legal responsibilities of health providers, and the potential of this sector to mitigate the consequences of violence. More recently, Sama carried out a review of existing practices in responding to child sexual abuse and found gaping holes in the response of Delhi hospitals. This evidence was used to advocate for the rigorous implementation of the medico-legal guidelines and protocols issued by the Ministry of Health and Family Welfare (MoHFW) after 2013. Sama has also been engaging the private sector, especially the Association of Obstetrics and Gynaecologists (AOGD) in New Delhi, to respond to sexual violence survivors. Sama continues to engage health providers across Delhi, Bihar, Odisha, and Jharkhand. Its advocacy campaigns have attempted to integrate the discourse on VAW into the agenda of health groups and, equally, to integrate the health impact discourse into the agenda of VAW groups and organisations.

Tathapi in Pune was established in 1999 as a women's health organisation to design health programmes to suit the local context of women's lives and to demand rational health services. As an active member of the Maharashtra chapter of the Jan Arogya Abhiyan (People's Health Movement), it was concerned about women's lack of access to healthcare as well as the impact of violence on the health of women. An important campaign led by Tathapi was on the "unnatural deaths" of women in the reproductive age group.

Maharashtra's *Vital Statistics* publication (1996) showed death by drowning and fire as the leading cause of unnatural deaths in women aged 15–45 years. Using such evidence, Tathapi was able to draw the attention of the Department of Health Services in Maharashtra to the need for a directive on documentation of a patient's history of domestic violence at primary health centres, but the health providers did not provide a comprehensive response. Noting the absence of training material for healthcare providers on the health consequences of VAW and ways to recognise them, Tathapi developed material in English and Marathi and trained doctors as well as front-line workers. The use of visuals ensured that the semi-literate could also understand the health consequences of VAW. Like Sama, Tathapi was aware that women often consult private healthcare providers and therefore developed sensitisation modules for them too. It also developed radio jingles, interactive material, and short films to bring the discourse into the mainstream.

Both Sama and Tathapi have kept their focus on the training of health providers in the public and private sector. They have not taken on service provision for survivors. Both have used research as a strategy quite effectively. Tathapi used data on unnatural deaths of women in the reproductive age group to raise awareness about VAW as a public health issue via a campaign with PHM India, while Sama documented gaps in the response to domestic violence and sexual violence in Delhi and other states.

Both organisations are active members of the PHM in India. Tathapi raised the issue with the assembly in 2000. However, despite the efforts of both groups, and other members of the PHM, the issue of VAW has remained on the periphery and not become a consistent demand of the PHM in India.

5.1 Sama – Resource Group for women and health

Deepa Venkatachalam and Adsa Fatima

Sama strengthens the knowledge, perspectives, and skills of healthcare providers in addressing gender-based violence.

Introduction

Sama's work on gender-based violence is rooted in its understanding of the close links between women's well-being and the other issues that affect their lives, such as food, livelihoods, and violence. Sama's early work on health with women and men from different regions and socioeconomic groups frequently highlighted the intimate relationship between violence and health. Whether these were processes with adivasi community activists, leaders (women and men) in Andhra Pradesh, or women leaders in Meghalaya, their voices contributed to Sama's understanding of gendered violence as a health issue. These interactions and processes further revealed that the violence that results from growing fundamentalism and the intersections of patriarchy, gender, caste, ethnicity, and religious identity has far-reaching consequences for physical and psychological health. Moreover, social institutions, including the healthcare system, have been historical as well as contemporary sites of violence. Women's narratives have exemplified the gendered, casteist perspectives and resultant unethical practices and violations by the healthcare system in its provisioning of "care." Sama's research over the years on population policies, contraceptive technologies, infertility, assisted reproductive technologies, and surrogacy has also underlined the biases of the health system.

Sama's active involvement in national platforms and coalitions such as the Jan Swasthya Abhiyan (JSA), the Indian chapter of the global People's Health Movement, and the Medico Friend Circle (MFC) has contributed to its increasingly nuanced understanding of the intersections of violence against women and health. JSA, according to its website, emerged in 2000 as a "worldwide movement to establish health and equitable development as top priorities through comprehensive primary healthcare and action on the social determinants of health." The JSA recognised that "mere access to healthcare, even if universal, will have no meaning unless the social determinants of health are addressed and issues of ethnicity, caste, class and gender are engaged with as a society."

Sama's involvement with issues of violence and health continues to be informed by these contexts and collectives. Although cognisant of the structural nature of VAW/G, Sama's engagement is situated in its broader work on strengthening comprehensive, gender-just, and equitable healthcare for all. While the absence of gender-just perspectives in the overall health system has been evident in the course of Sama's research, policy advocacy, and capacity-building on women's health issues, the marginalisation of certain health issues, including sexual and reproductive healthcare for young people and the provisioning of care and support for them, was particularly apparent. Gender-based violence was one such marginalised area that was not recognised sufficiently as a health issue by the health system or by the majority of organisations and networks working to strengthen the health system. This understanding, as well as spaces for collective initiatives with peer organisations, prompted Sama's systematic engagement with the health system in the context of VAW/G.

Strengthening capacities, building linkages

Sama's focused initiatives on GBV began in 2009 and were conceived at different levels: (i) at the level of healthcare facilities, (ii) at the level of organisations and networks working with diverse communities and issues across different states, and (iii) at the level of policy advocacy. Sama believes that working with the health system on VAW/G will strengthen the health system's broader perspectives on gender, sexuality, poverty, caste, disability, and religion. While engaging the health system on GBV, Sama was also aware of the challenges encountered in the public health system itself. These range from reduced investment in public health services and poor quality of human resources to the discrimination and violations manifest in state population policy mandates such as the two-child norm, which impacts access to healthcare.

Any comprehensive response by the health system in preventing and addressing GBV thus requires multi-sectoral action and linkages. Sama's initiatives include strengthening the knowledge, perspectives, and skills of healthcare providers (both public sector and private) in addressing GBV and responding to survivors of sexual and domestic violence (Sama 2013a).

These capacity-building initiatives are implemented jointly with healthcare institutions and medical colleges or independently by Sama. They are typically interactive orientations, either full-day or half-day, at healthcare facilities that reach out to different cadres of healthcare providers – doctors, nurses, and students across departments and specialisations – in the particular institution. These orientations strengthen perspectives on gender, violence, and ethics; emphasise the roles and responsibilities of the health system in the context of GBV; and update healthcare providers on relevant laws and policies. The orientations have underlined the mandated roles and accountability of the healthcare system and healthcare providers in responding to gender-based violence. The participating healthcare providers have in turn built capacities within their institutions and have been able to provide more informed care and support to survivors.

Consultations and seminars are also organised for healthcare providers working at different healthcare facilities. They provide a critical space to learn from experts and exchange experiences with peers on specific aspects of the health system's response to GBV. These consultations and seminars also provide collective and critical insights into the barriers and gaps that need to be addressed in the health system to enable a multi-sectoral response to VAW. Gaps in knowledge and perspectives on gender-based violence, lack of infrastructure and skilled human resources such as counsellors, limited skills in responding to survivors with disabilities and child survivors, and poor referral systems for the varied needs of survivors have emerged as some areas that need strengthening. The interface with the police, forensics laboratories, and judiciary is another challenge articulated during these dialogues.

The processes with community-based health workers such as ASHAs and Mitanins have been undertaken through discrete workshops in Chhattisgarh and other states. These workshops strengthen perspectives on gender, sexuality, and violence; facilitate information updates on law and ethics; and provide the fora for a collective stocktaking on responses to GBV.

Engaging the private health sector

Sama's engagement with private healthcare facilities is more recent. Sama conducts sessions at conferences of medical professional networks such as the Association of Obstetricians and Gynaecologists Delhi (AOGD) and state chapters of the Federation of Obstetrics and Gynaecological Societies of India (FOGSI). While there is increasing awareness amongst a limited number of private healthcare providers and facilities about the legal and policy mandates to provide care, including medico-legal care, there is still little clarity on how they should respond to GBV survivors. This is also the case with those facilitating access for survivors, including the police, and survivors themselves given the dominant perception that only the government healthcare system is required to respond to GBV.

Capacity-building efforts with healthcare providers have prompted their interest and motivation, as is evident from their proactive requests to Sama for advice, support, and clarifications on technical and legal issues. Hospitals have invited Sama to visit, review, and provide feedback on the systems and processes they have put in place. Others have been inclined to work with Sama to build the capacities of their peers through presentations and orientations at, for example, national and international conferences.

Working with community-based organisations

Sama has invested considerable time and effort in advancing the capacity of community-based organisations, networks, and members of health and other movements to understand GBV as a health issue. Organisations, networks, and health workers from Madhya Pradesh, Rajasthan, Delhi, Odisha, Bihar, Jharkhand, Chhattisgarh, Uttar Pradesh, Uttarakhand, Assam, Tripura, and Manipur have taken part in regional workshop processes over a three-year period, culminating in a national workshop that strengthened perspectives and capacities and created local interest and momentum. The participation of a range of activists working on diverse issues, such as women's health, livelihoods, Dalit rights, disabilities, mental health, and queer rights, has facilitated cross-learning and expanded the discourse around GBV. For instance, the experiences of GBV as well as the barriers in access to healthcare experienced by persons with disabilities, women in sex work, Dalit women, and trans persons have strengthened the capacity-building process. This cross-learning has also expanded Sama's understanding and work on gender-based violence, enabling linkages between health and GBV in different state contexts. For example, GBV in the context of conflict was an important part of the deliberations in Manipur and Chhattisgarh. In the former, articulations of domestic violence being subsumed by more visible forms of conflict and militancy flagged the need to better understand the connections between the two. In Odisha and Jharkhand, the need to understand the links between poverty, hunger, livelihoods, mining, and GBV was raised. In Jharkhand, the practice of witch-hunting and its deep connections with GBV was discussed. The regional workshops concluded with deliberations on strategies to engage with the health system on GBV in their respective states. While these workshops focused on building capacities and links between organisations as well as with the health system, national-level workshops and consultations were organised to share experiences of engagement with the health system, build momentum, and strengthen policy advocacy. These processes revealed the diverse strategies, opportunities, and challenges that different organisations experienced. While organisations and networks had begun to link with the health system at the block, district, and state levels, Sama saw the need for continued capacity-building of organisations, networks, and healthcare providers.

More recently, Sama has received requests from NGOs in other states to develop training frameworks for healthcare providers. One such request, for instance, has come from Chhattisgarh, where Sama has been working in collaboration with Chaupal, a Chhattisgarh-based organisation working on health and tribal rights issues. The initiative seeks to strengthen the health system response to gender-based violence and to initiate a decentralised health system response, from the community health worker to the tertiary health facility.

In an assessment carried out by Sama with government health facilities in Delhi in 2014, it was found that almost two dozen government health facilities in the capital have some systems in place to respond to survivors of GBV – sexual violence in particular. Strengthening these systems and processes through assessments, capacity-building, and policy advocacy has been a long-standing effort for Sama.

Along with capacity-building initiatives, Sama has been reviewing and monitoring the evolution of government policies, programmes, and protocols on GBV and informing the government of the ground realities and concerns (Sama 2013b). Sama has made recommendations to improve or strengthen proposed policy frameworks or protocols at the state and central levels, including recommendations to the J S Verma and Usha Mehra Committees, critical reviews and feedback on protocols for examination and evidence collection in sexual assault and one-stop crisis centres (Nirbhaya Centres), and the inclusion of VAW in election manifestos. Sama has made policy advocacy efforts, emphasising the accountability of the healthcare system in the provisioning of comprehensive ethical and gender-sensitive response, care, and treatment of survivors of gender-based violence.

Sama generally carries out consultative processes with multiple stakeholders to ensure that its recommendations at the level of policy or programme are nuanced and informed by existing realities. As an active member of the JSA, Sama has been flagging the discourse on GBV in the health movement at the national and global levels.

While the health system has a central role to play in GBV, any comprehensive response necessitates multi-sectoral linkages and coordinated referrals to enable survivors' access to legal aid, shelter, children's education, employment, skill-building, and so on. Sama has been facilitating such processes by exploring and linking to human and institutional resources (the sheer lack of resources and their abysmal quality, however, are a challenge).

The act of watching and influencing policies needs to be accompanied by an assessment of policy implementation or a review of the situation in which policies are to be implemented. Sama has been carrying out situational needs assessments and formative research on healthcare for GBV both at the level of healthcare facilities and at the community level. Such processes have provided critical insights into perspectives and gaps in knowledge and skills at different levels of the healthcare system. These assessments have not only brought deeply problematic processes to light but have also identified areas that need urgent attention and action. Recent assessments in Delhi and Chhattisgarh by Sama have revealed, for instance, the deep-rooted biases of the health system towards survivors – biases that prompt healthcare providers to assume false reporting in the majority of situations; blame women survivors, particularly those from socioeconomically marginalised communities, for the violence; and continue to perceive domestic violence as a "private matter." Other issues include the undue influence of the police or criminal justice system on medico-legal processes, which works in favour of powerful perpetrators of violence. These processes and learnings have been documented and disseminated to inform policy and protocols. Sama has also been developing other information resources such as posters to facilitate wider access to knowledge on GBV.

Thus, Sama's work in strengthening the healthcare response to GBV weaves together a range of strategies.

Going forward

Micro- and macro-level lessons have emerged over the years from Sama's work on GBV, providing several insights into strengthening engagements in this area. However, there has been no dearth of challenges and dilemmas either. Given the healthcare system's quick-fix approach to VAW, does it have the capacity or inclination to address VAW differently? What strategies would be required to develop a comprehensive approach? Where within the health system should the prevention of VAW fit? The prevention of VAW necessitates challenging existing unequal sociopolitical structures, and the healthcare system, with its vast outreach, is well placed to facilitate community-level action and support. However, in the absence of quality institutional support, community-level health workers remain isolated and exposed to risks in their interventions.

The present response to GBV by the health system, particularly in the medico-legal context, is disproportionately in favour of sexual violence rather than domestic violence. This may be in some ways linked to the previous discussion on the orientation of the health system. The medico-legal response – of examination, collection, and storage of samples and so on, in the case of sexual violence – is much more clear-cut and tangible than the response required for domestic violence. Challenging perspectives on domestic violence may require a higher level of people and counselling skills.

In the current scenario, the political economy of health is extremely relevant to any discussion on GBV. While on the one hand budget deficits and priorities point to the increasing withdrawal of the state, on the other the poor infrastructure and human resources in the healthcare system pose serious problems for any comprehensive and quality response to GBV.

The legal and policy space has witnessed some progressive steps in recent years: amendments in law through the Criminal Amendment Act (2013), the Protection of Women from Domestic Violence Act (PWDVA), the Protection of Children from Sexual Offences (POCSO) Act, and the medico-legal protocols on sexual violence issued by the Ministry of Health and Family Welfare (MoHFW). However, the implementation, for example, of the medico-legal protocols on sexual violence has been extremely poor, with minimal knowledge of their existence among healthcare institutions, organisations, and networks. These laws have also recognised and highlighted the role of health facilities in providing emergency medical treatment and psychological care to survivors of sexual violence and child sexual abuse. However, there is a huge gap between the action mandated by these legislations and the situation on the ground.

Another big concern has been the introduction of mandatory reporting of sexual violence by the health facility, which ends up hampering the survivor's right to seek treatment and care since survivors are often turned away and denied access to treatment by health facilities if they only wish to seek treatment and not lodge a police complaint. The provision of mandatory reporting, especially within the healthcare system, needs immediate review, as it jeopardises access to healthcare for survivors of sexual violence.

In addition, the healthcare response to VAW is generally available at the tertiary or secondary level of the healthcare system, creating isolated and selective spaces of care and thus creating serious barriers for access to healthcare in the context of GBV. These spaces also tend to be exclusive, with persons from marginalised groups being denied access or treated with disrespect and discrimination, further distancing them from the health system.

While there have been some extremely interested and involved persons in the healthcare system who have addressed GBV in difficult circumstances, responses are far from institutionalised. Therefore, organisations and networks working on the issue of GBV in the health system are very relevant.

References

Sama (2013a): *Assessment with public hospitals in Delhi*, New Delhi: Sama Resource Group for Women and Health.

Sama (2013b): *Gender based violence and health: Strengthening linkages and responses: An information booklet*, New Delhi: Sama Resource Group for Women and Health.

5.2 Tathapi

Audrey Fernandes

Tathapi enables the public and private health sectors in Maharashtra to respond to violence against women.

Introduction

Tathapi, a women and health resource centre set up in 1999, aims to equip marginalised communities to access healthcare services through a model of partnership with local and urban organisations across Maharashtra. It also aims to build the capacities of partnering organisations to research the health problems of communities and design women-centred health programmes to respond to local needs. Tathapi equips its partners to negotiate with the health system to demand rational health services. This case study presents the organisation's experience of engaging the health system (public and private) to respond to violence against women.

Tathapi is an active member of the Jan Arogya Abhiyan (JAA), a network of people's organisations, health organisations, women's collectives, and trade unions established in 2000 to bring attention to Health for All, the Alma Ata goal of 2000, to which India was also a signatory. One of JAA's concerns has been the neglect of women's health in general and the health consequences of violence in particular. JAA brought attention to the absence of an appropriate response to VAW by the health department. This resonated with Tathapi, which, in the course of its work on healthcare with communities, often heard women discussing the violence they faced. As part of the Maharashtra JAA, one of the areas Tathapi decided to address was violence against women and its impact on their health. The other areas were population policy, the two-child norm, and the falling sex ratio. Each of these areas of work was intrinsically connected to violence against women.

Tathapi initiated its work on VAW by using the data published by the state health department itself – the *Maharashtra Vital Statistics Handbook 1996* – on causes of death. The single most common cause of death amongst women in the reproductive age group (15–44 years) was burns, drowning, and suicide (Government of Maharashtra 1996), all of which are unnatural causes of death. Tathapi found that the falling sex ratio in Maharashtra showed a sharp decline in districts with better economic indicators (Government of India 2001). It found that the largely unregulated private sector was responsible for the misuse of sonography to detect female foetuses. These findings prompted Tathapi to build a case for working closely with the health system to develop strategies to respond to VAW within the JAA and through the JAA with the Government of Maharashtra's health department.

Objectives of working with the health sector

Tathapi's objective was to equip the health sector with the rationale and means to respond to violence against women from within. A campaign was initiated to increase awareness of VAW and its health consequences through the Maharashtra chapter of JAA and in collaboration with the Directorate of Health Services (DHS). Having the DHS on board indicated the sector's willingness to acknowledge VAW as a health issue. The DHS was ready to seek the expertise of the JAA in developing the means to respond to VAW.

While Tathapi pushed for recognition of violence against women as a public health issue, it also found it important to create tools to aid health providers in their response to VAW. Tathapi's engagement with the health sector on violence against women was a continuation of its efforts to operationalise the right to healthcare for marginalised communities.

Generating evidence and creating awareness

Tathapi developed a booklet in the local language as well as in English to generate in-depth discussion on VAW amongst health providers. It aimed to foster a dialogue on the health consequences of VAW amongst doctors, nurses, and women in the community, including elected panchayat members. A flip chart was designed for the benefit of semi-literate people. It presented the health consequences of violence through short case studies encountered at a PHC or hospital, such as women reporting mental illness, burns, or a sexually transmitted infection, the underlying cause of which was often the violence they faced. The flip chart provided steps to identify such health consequences and respond to them sensitively and comprehensively. Health professionals also used the chart to educate communities and community animators on seeking support and healthcare when faced with violence.

In addition, Tathapi collaborated with the Educational Media Research Centre (EMRC) to develop a short documentary for the education of doctors. This was broadcast on national television and was used in orientation sessions with doctors and nurses.

Engaging the public and private health system

Tathapi lobbied with JAA to engage the state department, which resulted in a government order (GO) directing medical officers at primary health centres in Maharashtra to record suspected and definite instances of violence against women. This meant that health providers were required to identify women facing violence, document the narration of violence, and provide treatment and care.

Tathapi then conducted trainings for nurses in the Pune Municipal Corporation (PMC) area on how to recognise and record the signs and symptoms of violence and provide basic support to patients: 236 nurses representing every clinic in the PMC region were trained in ten two-day workshops.

However, Tathapi was aware that women also reach out to the large private sector for treatment of the health consequences of violence. The Protection of Women from Domestic Violence Act (2005) places the legal responsibility for responding to the health consequences of VAW on both the public and private health sectors. POCSO 2012 and the Criminal Law Amendment (2013) also state that private health providers must attend to survivors of sexual violence immediately, providing them treatment and documenting the case.

Tathapi leveraged the PWDVA, which requires all health facilities (public and private) to provide women facing domestic violence immediate care and treatment. It conducted trainings and meetings to inform health providers about the law and refer them to a protection officer specially assigned by the law to provide support and services to women.

Tathapi was also instrumental in influencing the Indian Medical Association (IMA) to organise a panel discussion at the Maharashtra State Conference in 2005 to underline the role of doctors in the private sector in responding to VAW and stemming further decline in the sex ratio. The need for professional associations to take a firm stand against erring members was highlighted.

Key components of Tathapi's engagement with the health sector

Tathapi conducted 23 orientations with private sector doctors' associations in Pune and other districts of Maharashtra. These orientations were supported with posters that doctors could display at their clinics and a small booklet on available legal help, child support, and shelter homes for women. In addition, if a medical practitioner found a female patient needing immediate protection, tips were given on how this could be made possible (including hospital admission).

Tathapi realised that there is a need to create display material for both patients and health providers so that the issue of VAW and health is kept at the centre of health work. Tathapi's posters, creating awareness of seeking help and sharing information about violence with a health provider, continue to be displayed at several PHCs in Maharashtra.

After the trainings for health providers in the public and private sectors, Tathapi monitored the actual response of health providers. Dialogues with nurses showed that they had started using the communication skills provided to identify women and begun referring cases to organisations providing care and support.

PHC centres do not usually have provisions to record medico-legal cases, and suspected cases of violence are often referred to medical centres at higher levels, which are authorised to prepare a medico-legal report. However, women rarely went to record a medico-legal case at the higher medical centre. This prompted Tathapi to train PHC nurses to keep a record in their medical registers of women identified as facing violence and the support offered to them. This also helped create documentary evidence of the number of women identified by health providers. Between 2004 and 2006, 181 PHC staff in over 15 PHCs around Pune were trained to identify women facing violence and provide a sensitive response.

Tathapi created a radio jingle to create awareness among women about seeking medical care for issues of violence. It aired on All India Radio Pune for a month and received a good response, with women contacting Tathapi and seeking legal or medical help. Pamphlets explaining different forms of violence were distributed in the villages served by the 15 selected PHCs, which served to bring women in to talk about the violence they faced and its impact on their health.

The visits of a legal counsellor to the PHCs organised by Tathapi proved very helpful, underlining the need for counselling support at PHCs and rural hospitals.

Additionally, orientation activities on the interlinkages of violence against women and health were undertaken in 20 talukas.

The Tathapi model has thus comprised training of healthcare providers and monitoring of the activities carried out by them post training, enabling healthcare providers to initiate systematic documentation on identified VAW survivors and linking lawyers to PHCs when women require legal advice.

In addition, Tathapi was represented in the district monitoring of the Pre-Conception and Pre-Natal Diagnostic Techniques (PCPNDT) Act 1994, taking the lead in implementing and conducting sting operations on erring doctors. This created an environment of seriousness about VAW.

Gains and challenges

Innovations

Using health department data to highlight the issue of VAW over other health concerns such as maternal and reproductive healthcare brought out the epidemic proportions of VAW. Even the small acknowledgement through the government order by the DHS was a step towards acknowledging the gravity of the problem and the need for a response from health services.

Tathapi was also the first to engage with private sector doctors on VAW through their professional associations. This was done through systematic orientations at the taluka level and by inviting them to participate in creating protocols that they could implement at their clinics and private hospitals. In addition, private doctors were given special resources, including information booklets with telephone numbers of shelter homes and lawyers they could use to refer patients; pill packets for patients, with the names and phone numbers of organisations women could contact in case of emergency; and posters for display at their clinics.

Partnerships

Beyond the government order, working in partnership with the state to create a long-lasting impact on VAW from within the health services proved difficult. Aside from individual staffers who were sympathetic to the issue, sustaining the benefits and lessons learnt from the experiment was not possible. Change in leadership (district health officers and others) was also an impediment.

While individual doctors were willing to participate in exercises to create protocols, it was again difficult to get associations to take a stand on VAW. Though the IMA and FOGSI did pass resolutions against VAW – and sex selection in particular – during their state conferences in 2005, they shied away from taking action against erring doctors and implementing the protocols within their membership. While the work with the public and private sectors created a positive environment to address VAW, the unwillingness to implement protocols led, in a way, to a dead end. Advocacy at the highest levels was called for.

Lessons learnt

The first lesson learnt was that there is a definite need for VAW services within the health sector. There was a good response to the VAW services offered at the PHC level in rural areas. In other words, it is important to provide services (including legal advice) to identify, treat, and refer cases of VAW at the primary healthcare level. Such services benefited women. Advertising these services through radio jingles also made a huge difference.

Secondly, stronger advocacy at the state level is needed if healthcare for survivors of violence against women is to become a budget priority at the state level in line with the national programmes.

Building evidence of the health consequences of VAW is especially important. However, public sector personnel are reluctant to record cases in spite of the direction of the district health officers. Nurses would report cases, but this was not a priority for medical officers. For it to have validity, the effort for data collection must come from within the health sector itself. This decision can only come from the highest levels of the health sector.

References

Government of India (2001): *Census 2001*, New Delhi: Office of the Registrar General and Census Commissioner, Ministry of Home Affairs.

Government of Maharashtra (1996): "Causes of death among women in Maharashtra (rural)," in *Maharashtra vital statistics handbook*, pp. 15–44.

Section 6

Conclusion

This volume provides a consolidated account of public health approaches to violence against women and girls in India. The introduction presents an overview of the extent of VAW/G in the country and synthesises evidence of health system interventions to address the problem. The rest of the volume brings together hitherto unpublished case studies of health system responses in India to intimate partner/domestic violence and, to a lesser extent, sexual violence against women. There has been limited published information or research evidence of VAW interventions in the health system or their approaches, achievements, and challenges, and this has posed a barrier to learning from them. This volume fills the gap in evidence.

We have used our working knowledge of the field to identify the case studies for inclusion in this volume. Representatives of the organisations or health department concerned have written each case study, providing first-hand knowledge of the interventions. However, we noted an absence of systematic documentation and rigorous evaluation of almost all the interventions, a factor that limits the depth to which each case study can go. Despite this limitation, we believe the volume offers a comprehensive understanding of how health systems are addressing VAW in India, the major gaps in the health sector's response to VAW, and what needs to be done to move the agenda forward.

The interventions included vary in scope and scale; function in primary, secondary, and tertiary care institutions as well as at the community level; and have been led and implemented by NGOs or by the public health system, with varying degrees of collaboration between the two.

We classified the interventions into four main models, based on the level of integration with the public health system, from the most to the least integrated:

1 Interventions institutionalised by the public health system
2 NGO/CSO interventions within the public health system
3 Community-level health and related interventions by NGOs
4 Advocacy with the health sector to respond to VAW/G

Our classification of models bears some similarity to VAW/IPV interventions discussed in other studies. Colombini, Mayhew, and Watts (2008) proposed a classification of VAW/G interventions according to three levels of health sector integration: (i) provider/facility-level integration of select services, (ii) provider/facility-level integration of comprehensive services, and (iii) system-level integration involving multi-site linkages. Our Models 1 and 2 are integrating comprehensive services to survivors through facility-based departments, with linkages to other sectors such as the police, child welfare committees, courts, and shelters. The IPV interventions in South Asia reviewed by Pande et al. (2017) include interventions by the public health sector, interventions by women's collectives, and interventions via local government institutions. Our Models 3 and 4 include interventions implemented through women's collectives at the community level and by feminist NGOs with the health system. All four models appear to fall within the ambit of "advocacy interventions" (Trabold et al. 2018) – interventions in which a trained individual engages with the violence survivor and provides psychological first aid or counselling, referral to external resources, and harm reduction approaches such as safety planning.

The four models of intervention showcase some promising approaches to health-related services for women subjected to violence while also highlighting numerous limitations and challenges.

Evidence from studies around the globe shows that institutionalising a comprehensive health system response is among the most effective ways to address VAW/G (Rees, Zweigenthal, and Joyner 2014; Trabold et al. 2018). Model 1 (North East Network, Bhoomika, Sukoon, and Dilaasa) describes interventions by state governments in four Indian states to implement services for VAW/G survivors in secondary or tertiary care settings. They are among the small number of system-level interventions. They cater to a large population of women from marginalised groups and have been functional for several years. The states have issued guidelines for running these hospital-based departments, allocated resources, and designated staff for smooth functioning.

Model 2 (Vimochana, SNEHA, Soukhya, SWATI, and Anweshi) includes interventions introduced by NGOs within the public health sector. The NGOs have provided valuable services for many years, and even decades, benefitting hundreds of women. Skilled professional NGO staffs provide services for VAW/G at public health facilities. In all these interventions, the women using their services have benefitted from the NGOs' strong networks, which link them to additional resources, such as shelter, police, and legal support. Some of the NGOs that were grounded in feminist ideology have adopted an "empowerment" approach, encouraging autonomy and greater control and decision-making among survivors of violence. Other NGOs engaged in community-based activities have demonstrated successful referrals from the community to the VAW/G services located within public health facilities and follow-up of clients in the community thereafter. However, the lack of an institutional- or system-level policy on addressing VAW/G or clear protocols has placed the NGOs in an unenviable position. While the NGOs have had the support of the public health facility in carrying out their activities, they have had limited impact on changing the perspectives and clinical practices of healthcare providers. They have also had limited success in securing political support for integration of VAW/G services as an essential component of healthcare at the facilities where they are located, let alone within the public health sector as a whole.

The two case studies classified as Model 3 (MASUM and RUWSEC) are community-based interventions by women's collectives engaged in addressing women's health concerns that include VAW/G interventions as a component of a multi-faceted programme to improve women's health and well-being. Women's autonomy and empowerment are at the core of both interventions. Importantly, besides providing support to the violence survivor, both interventions have also worked to create an environment of zero tolerance of VAW/G through sustained education and mobilisation of women and men in the community. These case studies offer an approach distinct from those found in the literature on community-based VAW/G interventions in India. Pande et al. (2017), for instance, describe two types of interventions to address domestic violence by community-based collectives of marginalised women: (i) alternative dispute-resolution interventions in which public hearings are organised to bring the perpetrator to justice and (ii) the organisation of women into microfinance or self-help groups, which are not VAW/G interventions per se but are expected to lower women's risk of domestic violence by increasing their access to financial resources and social networks. Neither type has a focus on women's health or even a health component as part of the community-based intervention.

In both the case studies included under the third model, women survivors of violence who need physical and mental health services are, for the most part, referred to the organisation's own health centre. Women are also assisted in finding suitable welfare, police, and legal services. This provides important insights into how to create an ecosystem to prevent and respond to VAW/G at the community level.

Advocacy by NGO actors with the health sector through training of healthcare providers on VAW/G as a public health issue forms the core of our fourth model of intervention. The two case studies under this model (Sama and Tathapi) describe the array of educational programmes they have introduced for different levels of healthcare providers. These have ranged from one-off orientation sessions to a course with multiple knowledge- and skill-building sessions for medical doctors in the public and private sectors as well as public sector nurses and front-line workers. Both NGOs have made effective use of evidence to raise awareness and encourage the health sector to address VAW/G as a health issue. However, they have not gone beyond training and advocacy to monitoring changes in practice or to advocating for the creation of a facilitating environment within the health sector so that VAW/G interventions become possible.

While training of healthcare providers is the single most important focus of Model 4, training is also a component of all the other models. A successful institutional response to VAW should have in place a mechanism for ongoing training within the healthcare setting, with a core group of trainers at the facility level who are responsible for training and monitoring. Published evidence of VAW/G educational interventions with healthcare providers indicates the extent to which such interventions can motivate healthcare providers to identify and provide support for survivors. According to a scoping review of VAW/G educational interventions for healthcare professionals (Sprague et al. 2018) that included 65 published studies, 55% of the interventions had improved knowledge, skills, perceptions, and behaviours.

In the Indian context, VAW/G, including domestic violence and intimate partner violence, is conspicuously absent in the curricula for health professionals despite the growing body of evidence of how violence against women affects health conditions, health outcomes, and health-seeking behaviour. As a consequence, healthcare providers do not see themselves as having any role in addressing VAW/G, either as a clinical or as a public health issue. It does not help that we are socialised in a deeply hierarchical and patriarchal society and that disrespect and abuse of women are not uncommon within health facilities, especially in reproductive health services.

Maharashtra is the only state that has attempted to integrate gender into medical education, introducing VAW/G and sensitive response to survivors in the undergraduate medical curriculum. The curriculum was tested with medical students to assess their attitudes towards violence against women, revealing a significant positive change in the scores of medical students compared to baseline. These changes can be attributed to the fact that the health consequences of VAW/G and ways to address them are addressed in a foundation course as well as in the curriculum on medical examination of rape and medical termination of pregnancy (Rege et al. 2019).

The first three models, which include service-provisioning, provide services for survivors of intimate partner violence in heterosexual relationships and survivors of sexual violence – adults and children. However, violence against lesbian, gay, bisexual, trans, queer, and intersex (LGBTQI) persons, as well as sex workers, remains unaddressed. The MoHFW's 2014 medico-legal guidelines make an important contribution by laying down protocols for health professionals on responding to persons from various marginalised groups, such as the disabled, LGBTQI, sex workers, and so on. Unless sensitivity to these groups is built into the medical system, access to health services for marginalised groups will remain poor. There is evidence that health facilities are hostile to these groups, which prevents members of these marginalised communities from accessing healthcare. The gender in medical education initiative in Maharashtra has included sensitivity to and specific health concerns of the LGBTQI (Rege et al. 2019).

All four models described have focused primarily on responding to violence, although Model 3 also incorporates the prevention of violence. There has always been a debate about whether health system interventions should focus on preventing the occurrence of violence or on responding to violence. As the evidence and the models clearly demonstrate, health systems need to begin with the provision of supportive care because women approach health facilities for treatment and care following incidents of violence, but eventually they need to extend beyond clinical care.

An ideal health sector VAW intervention would be comprehensive, drawing on positive elements of all four models. In India, as in other low- and middle-income countries where resources are limited, there is a tendency to depend on NGOs to address VAW. Evidence from the Philippines and Malaysia, where NGOs were brought on board but could not provide long-term sustainable services, illustrates how NGOs and CSOs can partner in service-provisioning, training, technical support, capacity-building, research, monitoring, and evaluation, but the overall direction and management of the intervention should be centralised within the country's health systems (Bhate-Deosthali et al. 2018).

What we would like to see in place is a system-wide, institutionalised response to VAW in the health sector, with strong linkages to other sectors, including the NGO sector. An ideal model would provide services at various levels: identification and referral through front-line health workers and at PHCs and VAW services at the secondary and tertiary levels, with backward linkages to the primary care level. VAW services would be conceived as a multi-sectoral programme, with specific roles and responsibilities for different sectors and a multi-sectoral coordinating and monitoring mechanism accountable to the highest levels of governance. The links with NGOs would function at multiple levels. Front-line workers of the public health sector and PHCs would be linked to community-based organisations and would collaborate to create community support for zero tolerance of VAW/G as well as social support for survivors of violence. Secondary and tertiary care facilities would have formal collaborations with NGOs for training, technical support for women-centred approaches to VAW/G, and support for women being referred to welfare, police, and legal systems as well as for monitoring and evaluation.

Next steps

As a member of the UN, India is committed to the implementation of the Global Plan of Action issued in May 2014 at the 67th World Health Assembly on "strengthening the role of the health system in addressing violence, in particular against women and girls, and against children" (WHO 2016). The National Health Policy (Ministry of Health and Family Welfare 2017) reaffirmed this commitment to respond to violence against women. The policy states, "Women's access to healthcare needs to be strengthened by making public hospitals more women-friendly and ensuring that the staff have orientation to gender-sensitivity issues." The policy notes with concern the serious and wide-ranging consequences of VAW and recommends that free and sensitive healthcare to survivors/victims needs to be provided in the public and private health sectors.

The first step in operationalising the NHP commitment would be for the MoHFW to issue a national directive on addressing domestic/intimate partner violence and sexual violence. There is much scope for integration of a response to VAW in all health programmes, such as the National Health Mission and State Programme Implementation Plans. Learning from existing models of care, government should plan for a comprehensive and multi-sectoral programme in the health sector.

The second step would be to support the national directive with adequate financial resources for training of health professionals at all levels, appointment of counsellors in health facilities, coordination with the other sectors, and collaboration with NGOs.

The third step – and this is crucial – would be to invest in robust documentation, monitoring, and evaluation mechanisms so that one learns from the interventions as they unfold, correcting course as required. Such data need to be collected in a safe and confidential manner. Data must not be limited to quantitative information but also include qualitative data on client and provider perspectives.

Public education and interventions to bring about attitudinal change among key stakeholders are the other crucial areas of intervention that are essential for creating an environment of zero tolerance of violence.

Policy-oriented and implementation research on VAW/G interventions in the health sector in India is almost non-existent and cause for serious concern. We need research that is nuanced, does not treat all women survivors as a homogeneous group, and factors in the contexts in which interventions are implemented so that we know what works, for whom, and under what circumstances.

Realistic goals for health system interventions

An effective health system response to VAW/G can go a long way towards achieving the Sustainable Development Goals (SDGs) if the goals set are realistic and aligned with what the interventions can and cannot achieve.

VAW cannot be understood in terms of just individual and relationship factors. It is rooted in larger structural factors, and these same factors may also result in differential impact of violence on women from different social and economic groups. As indicated by many VAW prevention interventions, one of the major factors underlying male perpetration of violence against women is gender norms that support, excuse, or even encourage violence against women as an expression of masculinity. Policies and laws that result in limited access of women and girls to educational and work opportunities, unequal rights to property and within marriage, and constraints on their reproductive and sexual autonomy all contribute to women's vulnerability to domestic violence and limit their options for escaping a violent relationship.

Gender is embedded in social systems and institutions. Extreme poverty, class, caste, and gender inequalities and the resulting economic and social conditions of living – also known as "structural violence" – create and sustain conditions that shape gendered forms of violence, including interpersonal violence, in the lives of women in vulnerable social positions (Montesanti and Thurston 2015). Women's experience of violence and abuse is intertwined with factors such as the feminisation of poverty, transnational labour exploitation, and trade liberalisation resulting from market-oriented global economic policies (True 2010). Elimination of VAW, essential for the achievement of gender equality, is inextricably linked to the elimination of social and economic inequalities and the achievement of social justice.

While we recognise the need for change in these overarching structures, what we can hope to achieve from health sector interventions to address VAW is supportive and sensitive care for survivors of violence, mitigation of the negative health consequences of violence, empowerment of women to take effective action against violence, reduction of the recurrence of violence in the lives of individual women, and expansion of the support base for zero tolerance of violence.

References

Bhate-Deosthali P et al. (2018): *Role of the health sector in addressing intimate partner violence in India: A synthesis report*, New Delhi: International Centre for Research on Women.

Colombini, M, Mayhew, S and Watts, C (2008): "Health sector responses to intimate partner violence in low- and middle-income country settings: A review of current models, challenges and opportunities," *Bulletin of the World Health Organization*, Vol 86, No 8, pp. 635–642.

Ministry of Health and Family Welfare (2017): *National Health Policy 2017, India*, MoHFW Govt of India, New Delhi. Accessed from https://main.mohfw.gov.in/sites/default/files/9147562941489753121.pdf.

Montesanti, S R and Thurston, W E (2015): "Mapping the role of structural and interpersonal violence in the lives of women: Implications for public health interventions and policy," *BMC Women's Health*, Vol 15, Article 100.

Pande, R P et al. (2017): *Addressing intimate partner violence in South Asia: Evidence for interventions in the health sector, women's collectives, and local governance mechanisms*, New Delhi: International Centre for Research on Women.

Rees K, Zweigenthal V and Joyner, K (2014): "Health sector responses to intimate partner violence: A literature review," *African Journal of Primary Health Care & Family Medicine*, Vol 6, No 1, Article 712.

Rege, S et al. (2019): "Integrating gender perspectives in gynecology and obstetrics: Engaging medical colleges in Maharashtra, India," *International Journal of Gynecology and Obstetrics*, Vol 146, No 1, pp. 253–257.

Sprague, S et al. (2018): "A scoping review of intimate partner violence educational programs for healthcare professionals," *Women & Health*, Vol 58, No 10, pp. 1192–1206.

Trabold, N et al. (2018): "A systematic review of intimate partner violence interventions: State of the field and implications for practitioners," *Trauma, Violence and Abuse*, January 1.

True, J (2010): "The political economy of violence against women: A feminist international relations perspective," *Australian Feminist Law Journal*, Vol 32, No 1, pp. 39–59.

WHO (2016): *Global plan of action to strengthen the role of the health system within a national multisectoral response*, Geneva: World Health Organization.

Index

Note: Page numbers in *italics* indicate a figure and page numbers in **bold** indicate a table on the corresponding page.